The True T[ravels,]

Adventures, and Ob[servati]ons of

Captain John Smith into Europe,

Asia, Africa, and America

From Ann. Dom. 1593 to 1629

John Smith

Alpha Editions

This edition published in 2024

ISBN : 9789362517869

Design and Setting By
Alpha Editions
www.alphaedis.com
Email - info@alphaedis.com

As per information held with us this book is in Public Domain.
This book is a reproduction of an important historical work. Alpha Editions uses the best technology to reproduce historical work in the same manner it was first published to preserve its original nature. Any marks or number seen are left intentionally to preserve its true form.

Contents

CHAPTER. I. ....- 1 -
CHAPTER. II. ....- 3 -
CHAPTER. III. ....- 6 -
CHAPTER. IV. ....- 8 -
CHAPTER. V. ....- 10 -
CHAPTER. VI. ....- 12 -
CHAPTER. VII. ....- 14 -
CHAPTER. VIII. ....- 18 -
CHAPTER. IX. ....- 22 -
CHAPTER. X. ....- 25 -
CHAPTER. XI. ....- 27 -
CHAPTER. XII. ....- 29 -
CHAPTER. XIII. ....- 31 -
CHAPTER. XIIII. ....- 33 -
CHAPTER. XV ....- 35 -
CHAPTER. XVI. ....- 38 -
CHAPTER. XVII. ....- 41 -
CHAPTER. XVIII. ....- 44 -
CHAPTER. XIX. ....- 48 -
CHAPTER. XX. ....- 52 -
CHAPTER. XXI. ....- 54 -
CHAPTER. XXII. ....- 59 -
CHAPTER. XXIII. ....- 61 -
CHAPTER. XXIV. ....- 64 -
CHAPTER. XXV ....- 68 -
CHAPTER. XXVI. ....- 74 -

| CHAPTER. XXVII. | - 76 - |
| CHAPTER. XXVIII. | - 79 - |

CHAPTER. I.

His Birth; Apprenticeship; Going into France; *His beginning with Ten Shillings and three Pence; His Service in the* Netherlands; *His bad Passage into* Scotland; *His return to* Willoughby, *and how he lived in the Woods.*

HE WAS born in *Willoughby* in *Lincoln-shire,* and a Scholar in the two Free-Schools of *Alford* and *Louth.* His Father antiently descended from the ancient *Smiths* of *Crudley* in *Lancashire;* his Mother from the *Rickards* at Great *Heck,* in *York-shire.* His Parents dying when he was about Thirteen Years of Age, left him a competent Means, which he not being capable to manage, little regarded; his Mind being even then set upon brave Adventures, sold his Satchel, Books, and all he had, intending secretly to get to Sea, but that his Fathers Death stay'd him. But now the Guardians of his Estate more regarding it than him, he had liberty enough, though no Means, to get beyond the Sea. About the Age of Fifteen Years, he was bound an Apprentice to Mr. *Thomas Sendalt* of *Linne,* the greatest Merchant of all those Parts; but because he would not presently send him to Sea, he never saw his Master in Eight Years after. At last he found Means to attend Mr. *Peregrine Berty* into *France,* second Son to the Right Honourable *Peregrine,* that generous Lord *Willoughby,* and famous Soldier; where coming to his Brother *Robert,* then at *Orleans,* now Earl of *Lindsey,* and Lord Great Chamberlain of *England;* being then but little Youths under Tutorage: His Service being needless, within a Month or six Weeks they sent him back again to his Friends; who when he came from *London,* they liberally gave him (but out of his own Estate) Ten Shillings to be rid of him; such oft is the share of Fatherless Children: But those two Honourable Brethren gave him sufficient to return for *England.* But it was the least thought of his Determination, for now being freely at liberty in *Paris,* growing acquainted with one Mr. *David Hume,* who making some use of his Purse, gave him Letters to his Friends in *Scotland* to prefer him to King *James.* Arriving at *Roan,* he better bethinks himself, seeing his Money near spent, down the River he went to *Haver de grace,* where he first began to learn the Life of a Soldier: Peace being concluded in *France,* he went with Captain *Joseph Duxbury* into the Low-Countries, under whose Colours, having served three or four Years, he took his Journey for *Scotland,* to deliver his Letters. At *Ancusan* he imbark'd himself for *Lethe,* but as much danger, as Shipwreck and Sickness could endure, he had at the Holy Isle in *Northumberland* near Berwick, (being recovered) into *Scotland* he went to deliver his Letters. After much kind usage among those honest *Scots* at *Ripweth* and *Broxmoth,* but neither Money nor Means to make him a Courtier, he returned to *Willoughby* in *Lincoln-shire;* where within a short time, being glutted with too much

Company, wherein he took small delight, he retired himself into a little Woody Pasture, a good way from any Town, invironed with many hundred Acres of other Woods: Here, by a fair Brook he built a Pavillion of Boughs, where only in his Cloths he lay. His Study was *Machiavil's* Art of War, and *Marcus Aurelius;* his exercise a good Horse, with his Lance and Ring; his Food was thought to be more of Venison than any thing else; what he wanted his Man brought him. The Country wondering at such an Hermite, his Friends perswaded one Seignior *Theodora Polaloga,* Rider to *Henry* Earl of *Lincoln,* an excellent Horse Man, and a Noble *Italian* Gentleman, to insinuate into his Woodish Acquaintance, whose Languages and good Discourse, and Exercise of Riding drew him to stay with him at *Tattersall.* Long these Pleasures could not content him, but he returned again to the Low Countries.

CHAPTER. II.

The notable Villany of four French *Gallants, and his revenge;* Smith *thrown over-board;* Captain *La Roche of Saint* Malo *relieves him.*

THUS when *France* and *Netherlands* had taught him to Ride a Horse, and use his Arms, with such Rudiments of War, as his tender Years in those Martial Schools could attain unto; he was desirous to see more of the World, and try his Fortune against the *Turks*, both repenting and lamenting to have seen so many *Christians* slaughter one another. {MN} Opportunity calling him; into the Company of four *French* Gallants well attended, faining to him the one to be a great Lord, the rest his Gentlemen, and that they were all devoted that way; over-perswaded him to go with them into *France*, to the Dutchess of *Merceur*, from whom they should not only have Means, but also Letters of Favour to her Noble Duke, then General for the Emperour *Rolduphus* in *Hungary;* which he did, with such ill Weather as Winter affordeth, in the dark Night they arrived in the broad shallow In-let of St. *Valleries sur Soame* in *Picardie;* His *French* Lord knowing he had good Apparel, and better furnished with Money than themselves, so Plotted with the Master of the Ship, to set his and their own Trunks ashore, leaving *Smith* aboard till the Boat could return, which was the next day after, towards Evening: The reason he alledged, was, the Sea went so high he could come no sooner, and that his Lord was gone to *Amiens,* where they would stay his coming; which treacherous Villany, when divers other Soldiers, and Passengers understood, they had like to have slain the Master, and had they known how, would have run away with the Ship.

{MN} *A notable Villany of four* French *Gallants.*

Coming on shoar, he had but one *Cavvalue,* {MN-1} was forced to sell his Cloak to pay for his Passage. One of the Soldiers, called *Curzianvere*, compassionating his Injury, assured him, this great Lord *Depreau* was only the Son of a Lawyer of *Mortaigne* in base *Britany*, and his Attendants *Cursell, La Nelie,* and *Monserrat*, three young Citizens, as arrant Cheats as himself; but if he would accompany him, he would bring him to their Friends, but in the *interim* supplied his wants: Thus Travelling by *Deepe, Cadebeck, Humphla, Pountdemer* in *Normandy*, they came to *Caen* in base *Normandy;* where both this Noble *Curzianvere*, and the great Prior of the great Abbey of St. *Steven* (where is the ruinous Tomb of *William* the Conqueror) and many other of his Friends kindly welcomed him, and brought him to *Montaigne*, where he found *Depreau* and the rest, but to small purpose; for Mr. *Curzianvere* was a banished Man, and durst not be seen but to his Friends: yet the bruit of their Cozenage occasioned the Lady *Collumber*, the Baron *Larshan*, the Lord *Shasghe*, and divers other honourable Persons, to supply his wants, and with them to recreate him-self so long as he would; But such pleasant pleasures suited little with his poor Estate, and his restless Spirit, that could never find content, to receive such Noble Favours, as he could neither deserve nor requite: But wandering from Port to Port to find some Man of War, spent that he had, and in a Forest, near dead with grief and cold, a rich Farmer found him by a fair Fountain, under a Tree: This kind Peasant relieved him again to his content, to follow his intent. {MN-2} Not long after, as he passed thorow a great Grove of Trees, between *Pounterson* and *Dina* in *Britany*, it was his chance to meet *Cursell*, more miserable than himself: His piercing Injuries had so small patience, as without any word they both drew, and in a short time *Cursell* fell to the Ground, where, from an old ruinated Tower, the Inhabitants seeing them, were satisfied, when they heard *Cursell* confess what had formerly passed; and that how, in the dividing that they had stolen from him, they fell by the Ears amongst themselves, that were Actors in it; but for his part, he excused himself to be innocent as well of the one, as of the other. In regard of his hurt, *Smith* was glad to be so rid of him, directing his course to an honourable Lord, the Earl of *Ployer*, {MN-3} who during the War in *France*, with his two Brethren, Viscount *Poomory*, and Baron *d'Mercy*, who had been brought up in *England;* by him he was better refurnished than ever. When they had shewed him Saint *Malo* Mount, Saint *Michael*, *Lambal*, *Simbreack*, *Lanion*, and their own fair Castle of *Tuncadeck*, *Gingan*, and divers other places in *Britany* (and their British *Cornwaile*) taking his leave, he took his way to *Raynes*, the *Britains* chief City, and so to *Nants*, *Poyters*, *Rochel*, and *Bourdeaux*. The rumour of the strength of *Bayon* in *Biskay*, caused him to see it; and from thence took his way from *Leskar* in *Bicarne*, and *Paw*, in the Kingdom of *Navarre* to *Tolouza* in *Gascoigne*, *Bezers*, and *Carcassone*, *Narbone*, *Montpelier*, *Nimes* in *Languedeck*, and thorow the Country of *Avignion*, by *Aries* to *Marseilles* in *Provence*, there imbarking himself for *Italy;* the Ship was inforced to *Tolonne*, and putting again to Sea, ill Weather so grew upon them, that they Anchored close aboard the Shoar, under the little Isle of St. *Mary*, against *Nice* in *Savoy*. Here the inhuman Provincials, with a Rabble of Pilgrims of divers Nations going to *Rome*, hourly cursing him, not only for a *Hugonot* but his Nation they swore were all Pirats, and so vilely railed on his dread Soveraign Queen *Elizabeth*, and that they never should have fair Weather so long as he was aboard them; their Disputations grew to that Passion, that they threw him over board, yet God brought him to that little Isle, where was no Inhabitants, but a few Kine and Goats. The next Morning, he espied two Ships more riding by them, put in by the Storm, that fetched him aboard, well refreshed him, and so kindly used him, that he was well contented to try the rest of his Fortune with them. {MN-5} After he had related unto them his former

Discourse, what for pity, and the love of the Honourable Earl of *Ployer*, this Noble *Britain* his Neighbour, Captain *la Roche* of Saint *Malo*, regarded and entertained him for his well respected Friend. With the next fair Wind, they Sailed along by the Coast of *Corsica* and *Sardinia*, and crossing the Gulf of *Tunis*, passed by Cape *Bona* to the Isle of *Lempadosa*, leaving the Coast of *Barbary* till they came at *Cape Rasata*, and so along the *African* Shoar, for *Alexandria* in *Ægypt*. There delivering their Fraught, they went to *Seandaroone*, rather to view what Ships were in the Road, than any thing else: keeping their Course by *Cypres*, and the Coast of *Asia*, Sailing by *Rhodes*, the *Archipelagus*, *Candia*, and the Coast of *Grecia*, and the Isle of *Zefalonia*. They lay to and again a few days, betwixt the Isle of *Corsue*, and the Cape of *Orranto*, in the Kingdom of *Naples*, in the Entrance of the *Adriatick* Sea.

{MN-1} *A Cavvalue is in value a penny.*

{MN-2} *Here he incountred one of the thieves.*

{MN-3} *The Nobleness of the Earl of* Plover.

{MN-4} *An inhuman act of the Provincials in casting him overboard.*

{MN-5} *Capt.* La Roche *relieves him.*

CHAPTER. III.

A desperate Sea Fight in the Streights; His Passage to Rome, Naples, *and the view of* Italy.

BETWIXT the two *Capes*, they met with an *Argosie* of *Venice*; it seemed the Captain desired to speak with them, whose untoward answer was such, as slew them a Man; {MN} whereupon the *Britain* presently gave them the Broad-side, then his Stern, and his other Broad-side also, and continued the Chase, with his chase Pieces, till he gave them so many Broad-sides one after another, that the *Argosies* Sails and Tackling was so torn, she stood to her defence, and made shot for shot; twice in one hour and a half the *Britain* boarded her, yet they cleared themselves, but clapping her aboard again, the *Argosie* fired him, which with much danger to them both was presently quenched. This rather augmented the *Britain's* rage, than abated his courage; for having reaccommodated himself again, shot her so oft between Wind and Water, she was ready to sink, then they yielded; the *Britain* lost fifteen Men, she twenty, besides divers were hurt, the rest went to Work on all hands; some to stop the Leaks, others to guard the Prisoners that were chained, the rest to ride her. The Silks, Velvets, Cloth of Gold, and Tissue, Piasters, Chicqueens and Sultanies, which is Gold and Silver, they unloaded in four and twenty hours, was wonderful, whereof having sufficient, and tired with toil, they cast her off with her Company, with as much good Merchandize as would have fraughted such another *Britain*, that was but two Hundred Tuns, she four or five Hundred.

{MN} *A desperate Sea Fight.*

To repair his Defects, he stood for the Coast of *Calabria*, but hearing there was six or seven Galleys at *Messina*, he departed thence for *Malta;* but the Wind coming fair, he kept his course along the Coast of the Kingdom of *Sicilia*, by *Sardinia* and *Corsica*, till he came to the Road of *Antibo* in *Peamon*, where he set *Smith* on shoar with five Hundred Chicqueens, and a little Box God sent him worth near as much more. Here he left this Noble *Britain*, and embarked himself for *Legorn*, being glad to have such opportunity and means to better his Experience by the view of *Italy;* and having passed *Tuskany*, and the Country of *Siena*, where he found his dear Friends, the two Honourable Brethren, the Lord *Willoughby*, and his Brother cruelly wounded, in a desperate fray, yet to their exceeding great Honour. Then to *Viterbo* and many other Cities he came to *Rome*, from where it was his chance to see Pope Clement the VIII. with many Cardinals, creep up the Holy Stairs, {MN} which they say, are those our Savior Christ went up to *Pontius Pilate*, where blood, falling from his Head, being pricked with his Crown of Thorns, the drops are marked with Nails of Steel, upon them none dare go but in that manner, saying so many *Ave-Maries* and *Pater-Nosters*, as is their Devotion, and to kiss the Nails of Steel: But on each side, is a pair of such like Stairs, upon which you may go, stand, or kneel, but divided from the Holy Stairs by two Walls: Right against them is a Chappel, where hangs a great Silver Lamp, which burneth continually; yet they say, the Oil neither increaseth nor diminisheth. A little distant is the ancient Church of Saint *John de Lateran*, where he saw him say Mass, which commonly he doth upon some Friday once a Month. Having saluted Father *Parsons*, that famous *English* Jesuit, and satisfied himself with the Rarities of *Rome*, he went down the River of *Tiber* to *Civita Vechia*, where he embarked himself, to satisfie his Eye with the fair City of *Naples*, and her Kingdoms Nobility; returning by *Capua*, *Rome* and *Siena*, he passed by that admired City of *Florence*, the Cities and Countreys of *Bolonia*, *Ferrara*, *Mantua*, *Padua* and *Venice*, whose Gulf he passed from *Malamoco* and the *Adriatic* Sea for *Ragouza*, spending some time to see that barren, broken Coast of *Albania* and *Dalmatia*, to *Capo de Istria*, Travelling the main of poor *Sclavonia* by *Lubbiano*, till he came to *Grates* in *Styria*, the Seat of *Ferdinando*, Arch-duke of *Austria*, now Emperour of *Almania:* where he met an *English* Man, and an *Irish* Jesuit, who acquainted him with many brave Gentlemen of good Quality, especially with the Lord *Ebersbaught*, with whom, trying such Conclusions, as he projected to undertake, preferred him to Baron *Kisell*, General of the Artillery, and he to a worthy Colonel, the Earl of *Meldritch*, with whom, going to *Vienna* in *Austria*, under whose Regiment, in what Service, and how he spent his time, this ensuing Discourse will declare.

{MN} *The Popes holy stairs brought from* Jerusalem, *whereon (they say) Christ went up to* Pontius Pilate.

CHAPTER. IV.

The Siege of Olumpagh; *An excellent Stratagem by* Smith; *Another not much worse.*

AFTER the loss of *Caniza*, the *Turks* with Twenty thousand besieged the strong Town of *Olumpagh* so straitly, as they were cut off from all intelligence and hope of succour; till *John Smith*, this *English* Gentleman, acquainted Baron *Kisell*, General of the Arch-dukes Artillery, he had taught the Governour, his worthy Friend, such a Rule, that he would undertake to make him know any thing he intended, and have his answer, would, they bring him but to some place where he might make the Flame of a Torch seen to the Town; *Kisell* inflamed with this strange Invention, *Smith* made it so plain, that forthwith he gave him Guides, who in the dark Night brought him to a Mountain, where he shewed three Torches equidistant from the other, which plainly appearing to the Town, the Governour presently apprehended, and answered again with three Other fires in like manner; each knowing the others being and intent; *Smith*, though distant seven Miles, signified to him these Words: *On Thursday at Night I will charge on the East, at the Alarum, salley you;* Ebersbaught answered, *he would,* and thus it was done: First he writ his Message as brief, you see, as could be, then divided the Alphabet into two parts thus;

A. b. c. d. e. f. g. h. i. k. l. I. I. I. I. I. I. I. I. I. I. I. m. n. o. p. q. r. s. t. v. w. x. 2. 2. 2. 2. 2. 2. 2. 2. 2. 2. 2. y. z. 2. 2.

{MN} *The siege of* Olumpagh.

{M-1} The first part from *A.* to *L.* is signified by shewing and hiding one link, so oft as there is Letters from *A.* to that Letter you mean; the other part from *M.* to *Z.* is mentioned by two Lights in like manner. The end of a Word is signified by shewing of three Lights, ever staying your Light at that Letter you mean, till the other may write it in a Paper, and answer by his signal, which is one Light, it is done, beginning to count the Letters by the Lights, every time from *A.* to *M.* by this means also the other returned his answer, whereby each did understand other. The Guides all this time having well viewed the Camp, returned to *Kisel,* who, doubting of his power, being but Ten thousand, was animated by the Guides, how the *Turks* were so divided by the River in two parts, they could not easily second each other. {MN-2} To which *Smith* added this conclusion; that two or three thousand pieces of Match fastened to divers small Lines of an hundred Fathom in length, being armed with Powder, might all be fired and stretched at an instant before the

Alarum, upon the Plain, of *Hysnaburg,* supported by two Staves, at each lines end, in that manner would seem like so many Musketeers; which was put in Practice; and being discovered by the *Turks,* they prepared to encounter these false fires, thinking there had been some great Army: whilst *Kisel* with his Ten thousand being entred the *Turks* quarters, who ran up and down as Men amazed, it was not long ere *Ebersbaught* was pell-mell with them in their Trenches; in which distracted confusion, a third part of the Turks that besieged that side towards *Knowsbruck,* were slain; many of the rest drowned, but all fled. The other part of the Army was so busied to resist the false fires, that *Kisel* before the Morning put two thousand good Soldiers in the Town, and with small loss was retired; the Garrison was well relieved with what they found in the *Turks* Quarters, which caused the *Turks* to raise their Siege and return to *Caniza:* and *Kisel* with much honour was received at *Kerment,* and occasioned the Author a good Reward and Preferment, to be Captain of Two hundred and fifty Horse-men, under the conduct of Colonel *Voldo,* Earl of *Meldritch.*

{MN-1} *An excellent Stratagem.*

{MN-2} *Another stratagem.*

CHAPTER. V.

The Siege of Stoll-weissenburg; *The effects of* Smith's *Fire-works; A worthy Exploit of Earl* Rosworme; *Earl* Meldritch *takes the* Bashaw *Prisoner.*

A GENERAL rumour of a general Peace, now spred it self over all the face of those tormented Countries: but the *Turk* intended no such matter, but levied Soldiers from all Parts he could. The Emperour also, by the assistance of the *Christian* Princes, provided three Armies, the one led by the Arch-duke *Matthias*, the Emperour's Brother, and his Lieutenant Duke *Merceur* to defend Low *Hungary;* the second, by *Ferdinando* the Arch-duke of *Styria,* and the Duke of *Mantua* his Lieutenant to regain *Caniza;* the third by *Gonzago*, Governour of High *Hungary,* to joyn with *Georgio Buson* to make an absolute conquest of *Transilvania.*

Duke *Merceur* with an Army or Thirty thousand, whereof near Ten thousand were *French,* besieged *Stoll-weissenburg,* otherwise called *Alba Regalis,* a place so strong by Art and Nature, that it was thought impregnable. At his first coming, The *Turks* sallied upon the *German* Quarter, slew near five hundred, and returned before they were thought on. The next Night in like manner, they did near as much to the *Bemers,* and *Hungarians;* of which, Fortune still presuming, thinking to have found the *French* quarter as careless, Eight or Nine hundred of them were cut in pieces and taken Prisoners. In this Encounter Monsieur *Grandvile,* a brave *French* Colonel, received seven or eight cruel Wounds, yet followed the Enemy to the Ports; he came off alive, but within three or four days died.

{MN} *The siege of* Alba Regalis.

Earl *Moldritch,* by the Information of of three or four *Christians,* (escaped out of the Town) upon every Alarum, where there was greatest Assemblies and throng of People, {MN} caused Captain *Smith* to put in practice his fiery Dragons, he had demonstrated unto him, and the Earl *Von Sulch* at *Comora* which he thus performed: Having prepared forty or fifty round-bellied Earthen Pots, and filled them with hand Gun powder, then covered them with Pitch, mingled with Brimstone and Turpentine; and quartering as many Musket-bullets, that hung together but only at the Center of the division, stuck them round in the mixture about the Pots, and covered them again with the same mixture, over that a strong Searcloth, then over all, a good thickness of Towze-match, well tempered with Oyl of Lin-seed, Camphire, and Powder of Brimstone, these he fitly placed in Slings, graduated so near as they could to the places of these Assemblies. At mid-night upon the Alarum, it was a fearful sight to see the short flaming course of their flight in the Air, but presently after their fall, the lamentable noise of the miserable slaughtered *Turks* was most wonderful to hear: Besides, they had fired that Suburb at the Port of *Buda* in two or three places, which so troubled the *Turks* to quench, that had there been any means to have assaulted them, they could hardly have resisted the fire, and their Enemies. The Earl *Rosworme*, contrary to the opinion of all Men, would needs undertake to find means to surprize the Segeth and Suburb of the City, strongly defended by a muddy Lake, which was thought unpassable.

{MN} *The effect of good fireworks.*

The Duke having planted his Ordnance, battered the other side, {MN-1} whilst *Rosworme* in the dark Night, with every Man a bundle of Sedge and Bavins still thrown before them, so laded up the Lake, as they surprised that unregarded Suburb before they were discovered: Upon which unexpected Alarum, the *Turks* fled into the City, and the other Suburb not knowing the matter, got into the City also, leaving their Suburb for the Duke, who, with no great resistance, took it, with many Pieces of Ordnance; the City, being of no such strength as the Suburbs, with their own Ordnance was so battered, that it was taken by force, with such a merciless Execution, as was most pitiful to behold. {MN-2} The *Bashaw* notwithstanding, drew together a Party of Five hundred before his own Palace, where he intended to die; but seeing most of his Men slain before him, by the valiant Captain, Earl *Meldritch*, who took him Prisoner with his own hands; and with the hazard of himself saved him from the fury of other Troops, that did pull down his Palace, and would have rent him in pieces, had he not been thus preserved. The Duke thought his Victory much honoured with such a Prisoner; took order, he should be used like a Prince, and with all expedition gave charge presently to repair the Breaches, and the Ruins of this famous City, that had been in the possession of the *Turks* near threescore years.

{MN-1} *A worthy Exploit of Earl* Rosworme.

{MN-2} *Earl* Meldritch *takes the* Bashaw *prisoner.*

CHAPTER. VI.

A brave Encounter of the Turks *Army with the* Christians; *Duke* Merceur *overthroweth* Assan Bashaw; *He divides the* Christian *Army; His Nobleness and Death.*

MAHOMET the Great *Turk*, during the Siege, had raised an Army of Sixty thousand Men to have relieved it; but hearing it was lost, he sent *Assan Bashaw*, General of his Army, the *Bashaw* of *Buda, Bashaw Amaroz*, to see if it were possible to regain it; The Duke understanding there could be no great experience in such a new levied Army as *Assan* had, having put a strong Garrison into it, and with the brave Colonel *Rosworme, Culnits, Meldritch*, the *Rhine Grave, Vahan,* and many others, with Twenty thousand good Soldiers, set forward to meet the *Turk,* in the Plains of *Girk.* {MN-1} Those two Armies encountred as they marched, where began a hot and bloody Skirmish betwixt them, Regiment against Regiment, as they came in order, till the night parted them: Here Earl *Meldritch* was so invironed among those half circular Regiments of *Turks,* they supposed him their Prisoner, and his Regiment lost; but his two most couragious Friends, *Vahan* and *Culnits,* made such a Passage amongst them, that it was a terror to see how Horse and Man lay sprawling and tumbling, some one way, some another on the Ground. The Earl there at that time made his valour shine more bright than his Armour, which seemed then painted with *Turkish* Blood; he slew the brave *Zanzack Bugola*, and made his Passage to his Friends, but near half his Regiment was slain. Captain *Smith* had his Horse slain under him, and himself sore wounded; but he was not long unmounted, for there was choice enough of Horses, that wanted Masters. The *Turk,* thinking the Victory sure against the Duke, whose Army, by the Siege and the Garrison, he had left behind him, was much weakened, would not be content with one, but he would have all; and lest the Duke should return to *Alba Regalis,* he sent that Night Twenty thousand to besiege the City, assuring them, he would keep the Duke or any other from relieving them. Two or three days they lay each by other, entrenching themselves; the *Turks* daring the Duke daily to a sett Battle, {MN-2} who at length drew out his Army, led by the *Rhine-Grave, Culnits,* and *Meldritch* who upon their first Encounter, charged with that resolute and valiant courage, as disordered not only the foremost Squadrons of the *Turks,* but enforced all the whole Army to retire to the Camp, with the loss of five or six thousand, with the *Bashaw* of *Buda,* and four or five *Zanzacks,* with divers other great Commanders, Two hundred Prisoners, and nine pieces of Ordnance. At that instant appeared, as it were, another Army coming out of a Valley over a plain Hill, that caused the Duke at that time to be contented, and to retire to his Trenches; which gave time to *Assan,* to reorder his disordered Squadrons:

Here they lay nine or ten days, and more Supplies repaired to them, expecting to try the event in a sett Battle; but the Soldiers on both Parties, by reason of their great Wants, and approach of Winter, grew so discontented, that they were ready of themselves to break up the Leager; the *Bashaw* retiring himself to *Buda,* had some of the Rear Troops cut off. *Amaroz Bashaw* hearing of this, found such bad welcome at *Alba Regalis,* and the Town so strongly repaired with so brave a Garrison, raised his Siege, and retired to *Zigetum.*

{MN-1} *A brave encounter of the* Turks *Army with the* Christians.

{MN-2} *Duke* Merceur *overthroweth* Assan Bassa.

The Duke understanding, that the Archduke *Ferdinando,* had so resolutely besieged *Caniza* as what by the loss of *Alba Regalis,* and the *Turks* retreat to *Buda,* being void of hope of any relief, doubted not, but it would become again the *Christians.* {MN-1}To the furtherance whereof, the Duke divided his Army into three parts. The Earl of *Rosworme* went with Seven thousand to *Caniza,* the Earl of *Meldritch* with Six thousand he sent to assist *Georgio Busca* against the *Transilvanians,* the rest went with himself to the Garrisons of *Strigonium* and *Komara;* having thus worthily behaved himself, he arrived at *Vienne,* where the Arch-dukes and the Nobility with as much honour received him, as if he had conquered all Hungaria; his very Picture they esteemed would make them fortunate, which thousands kept as curiously as a precious relique. To requite this honour, preparing himself to return into *France,* to raise new Forces against the next year, with the two Arch-dukes, *Matthias* and *Maximilian,* and divers others of the Nobility, was with great Magnificence conducted to *Nurenburg,* there by them royally feasted, (how it chanced is not known;) {MN-2} but the next Morning he was found dead, and his Brother in Law died two days after; whose hearts, after this great Triumph, with much sorrow were carried into *France.*

{MN-1} *Duke* Merceur *divideth his army.*

{MN-2} *Duke* Merceur *and his brother in law die suddenly.*

CHAPTER. VII.

The unhappy Siege of Caniza; *Earl* Meldritch *serveth Prince* Sigismundus; *Prince* Moyses *besiegeth* Regall; Smith's *three single Combats; His Patent from* Sigismundus, *and Reward.*

{MN} THE WORTHY Lord *Rosworme* had not worse Journey to the miserable Siege of *Caniza,* (whereby the extremity of an extraordinary continuing Tempest of Hail, Wind, Frost and Snow, insomuch that the *Christians* were forced to leave their Tents and Artillery, and what they had; it being so cold, that three or four hundred of them were frozen to Death in a Night, and two or three thousand lost in that miserable flight in the Snowy Tempest, though they did know no Enemy at all to follow them) than the Noble Earl of *Meldritch* had to *Transilvania,* where hearing of the Death of *Michael,* and the brave Duke *Merceur,* and knowing the Policy of *Busca,* and the Prince his Royalty, being now beyond all belief of Men, in Possession of the best part of *Transilvania,* perswaded his Troops, in so honest a Cause, to assist the Prince against the *Turk,* rather than *Busca* against the Prince.

{MN} *The unhappy siege of* Caniza.

{MN} The Soldiers being worn out with those hard Pays and Travels, upon hope to have free liberty to make booty upon what they could get Possession of from the *Turks,* were easily perswaded to follow him whithersoever. Now this Noble Earl was a *Transilvanian* born, and his Fathers Country yet Inhabited by the *Turks;* for *Transilvania* was yet in three Divisions, though the Prince had the Hearts both of Country and People; yet the Frontiers had a Garrison amongst the unpassable Mountains, some for the Emperour, some for the Prince, and some for the *Turk:* To regain which small Estate, he desired leave of the Prince to try his Fortunes, and to make use of that experience, the time of twenty years had taught him in the Emperours service, promising to spend the rest of his days, for his Countrys defence in his Excellencies Service. The Prince glad of so brave a Commander, and so many expert and ancient Soldiers, made him Camp Master of his Army, gave him all necessary relief for his Troops, and what freedom they desired to plunder the *Turks.*

{MN} *Earl* Meldritch *serveth with Prince* Sigismundus.

{MN-1} The Earl having made many Incursions into the Land of *Zarkan,* among those Rocky Mountains, where were some *Turks,* some *Tartars,* but most *Bandittoes, Rennegadoes,* and such like, which sometimes he forced into the Plains of *Regall* where is a City, not only of Men and Fortifications, Strong of it self, but so environed with Mountains, that made the Passages so difficult, that in all these Wars, no attempt had been made upon it to any purpose: Having satisfied himself with the Situation, and the most convenient Passages to bring his Army into it: The Earth no sooner put on her green Habit, than the Earl overspread her with his armed Troops. To possess himself first of the most convenient Passage, which was a narrow Valley betwixt two high Mountains; he sent Colonel *Veltus* with his Regiment; dispersed in Companies to lie in *Ambuscado,* as he had directed them, and in the Morning to drive all the Cattel they could find before a Fort in that Passage, whom he supposed would sally, seeing but some small Party to recover their prey; which took such good success, that the Garrison was cut off by the *Ambuscado,* and *Veltus* seized on the Skonces, which were abandoned. *Meldritch* glad of so fortunate a beginning, it was six days ere he could with six thousand Pioneers make passage for his Ordnance: The *Turks* having such warning, strengthened the Town so with Men and Provision, that they made a scorn of so small a number as *Meldritch* brought with him before the City, which was but eight thousand. Before they had pitched their Tents, the *Turks* sallied in such abundance, as for an hour, they had rather a bloody Battel than a Skirmish, but with the loss of near Fifteen hundred on both sides. The Turks were chased till the Cities Ordnance caused the Earl to retire. {M-2} The next day *Zachel Moyses,* General of the Army, pitched also his Tents with nine thousand Foot and Horse, and six and twenty Pieces of Ordnance; but in regard of the Situation of this strong Fortress, they did neither fear them nor hurt them, being upon the point of a fair Promontory, environed on the one side within half a Mile with an un-useful Mountain, and on the other side with a fair Plain, where the *Christians* encamped, but so commanded by their Ordnance, they spent near a Month in entrenching themselves, and raising their Mounts to plant their Batteries; which slow proceedings the *Turks* oft derided, that their Ordnance were at pawn, and how they grew fat for want of Exercise, and fearing lest they should depart ere they could assault their City, sent this Challenge to any Captain in the Army.

{MN-1} *Earl* Meldritch *maketh incursions to discover* Regall.

{MN-2} Moyses *Besiegeth* Regal.

That to delight the Ladies, who did long to see some Court-like pastime, the Lord *Turbashaw* did defie any Captain, that had the command of a Company, who durst Combate with him for his Head: The matter being discussed, it was accepted, but so many Questions grew for the undertaking, it was decided by Lots, which fell upon Captain *Smith*, before spoken of.

{MN} Truce being made for that time, the Rampires all beset with fair Dames, and Men in Arms, the *Christians* in *Battalia; Turbashaw* with a noise of Haut-boys entred the Field well mounted and armed; on his shoulders were fixed a pair of great Wings, compacted of Eagles Feathers, within a ridge of Silver, richly garnished with Gold and precious Stones, a *Janizary* before him, bearing his Lance, on each side another leading his Horse; where long he stayed not, ere *Smith* with a noise of Trumpets, only a Page bearing his Lance, passing by him with a courteous Salute, took his Ground with such good success, that at the sound of the charge, he passed the *Turk* thorow the sight of his Beaver, Face, Head and all, that he fell dead to the Ground, where alighting and unbracing his Helmet, cut off his Head, and the *Turks* took his Body; and so returned without any hurt at all. The Head he presented to the Lord *Moyses*, the General, who kindly accepted it, and with joy to the whole Army he was generally welcomed.

{MN} *Three single combates.*

The Death of this Captain so swelled in the Heart of one *Grualgo,* his vowed Friend, as rather inraged with madness than choler, he directed a particular challenge to the Conqueror, to regain his Friends Head, or lose his own, with his Horse and Armour for advantage, which according to his desire, was the next day undertaken: as before upon the sound of the Trumpets, their Lances flew in pieces upon a clear Passage, but the *Turk,* was near unhorsed. Their Pistols was the next, which marked *Smith* upon the Placard; but the next shot the *Turk,* was so Wounded in the left Arm, that being not able to rule his Horse, and defend himself, he was thrown to the ground, and so bruised with the fall, that he lost his Head, as his Friend before him, with his Horse and Armour; but his Body, and his rich Apparel were sent back to the Town.

Every day the *Turks* made some Sallies, but few Skirmishes would they endure to any purpose. Our Works and Approaches being not yet advanced to that heighth and effect, which was of necessity to be performed; to delude time, *Smith* with so many incontradictible perswading Reasons, obtained leave, that the Ladies might know he was not so much enamoured of their Servants Heads; but if any *Turk,* of their rank would come to the place of Combate to redeem them, should have his also upon the like conditions, if he could win it.

The challenge presently was accepted by *Bonny Mulgro*. The next day, both the Champions entring the Field as before, each discharging their Pistol, having no Lances, but such martial Weapons as the Defendant appointed, no hurt was done; their Battle-Axes was the next, whose piercing Bills made sometime the one, sometime the other to have scarce sense to keep their Saddles, specially the *Christian* received such a blow, that he lost his Battle axe, and failed not much to have fallen after it, whereat the supposed conquering *Turk*, had a great shout from the Rampires. The *Turk*, prosecuted his advantage to the uttermost of his power; yet the other, what by the readiness of his Horse, and his judgement and dexterity in such a business, beyond all Mens expectation, by God's assistance, not only avoided the *Turks* violence but having drawn his Faulchion, pierced the *Turk*, so under the Culets, thorow back and body, that altho' he alighted from his Horse, he stood not long ere he lost his Head, as the rest had done.

CHAPTER. VIII.

Georgio Busca *an* Albane, *his ingratitude to Prince* Sigismundus; *Prince* Moyses *his Lieutenant, is overthrown by* Busca, *General for the Emperour* Rodulphus; Sigismundus *yieldeth his Country to* Rodulphus; Busca *assisteth Prince* Rodol *in* Wallachia.

THIS GOOD success gave such great encouragement to the whole Army, that with a Guard of six thousand, three spare Horses, before each a *Turks* Head upon a Lance, he was conducted to the Generals Pavilion with his Presents. Moyses received both him and them, with as much respect as the occasion deserved, embracing him in his Arms, gave him a fair Horse, richly furnished, a Scimitar and Belt worth Three hundred Ducats; and *Meldritch* made him Sergeant Major of his Regiment. But now to the Siege, having mounted six and twenty pieces of Ordnance, fifty or sixty Foot above the Plain, made them so plainly tell his meaning, that within fifteen days two Breaches were made, which the *Turks* as valiantly defended as Men could; that day was made a darksome Night, but by the light that proceeded from the murdering Muskets, and peace-making Canon, whilst their slothful Governour lay in a Castle on the top of a high Mountain, and like a Valiant Prince asketh what's the matter, when horror and death flood amazed each at other, to see who should prevail to make him victorious: {MN} *Moyses* commanding a general assault upon the sloping front of the high Promontory, where the Barons of *Budendorfe* and *Oberwin,* lost near half their Regiments, by Logs, Bags of Powder, and such like, tumbling down the Hill, they were to mount ere they could come to the breach; notwithstanding with an incredible courage, they advanced to the push of the Pike with the Defendants, that with the like courage repulsed, till the Earl *Meldritch, Becklefield* and *Zarvana,* with their fresh Regiments seconded them with that fury, that the *Turks* retired and fled into the Castle, from whence by a Flag of truce they desired composition. The Earl remembering his Fathers Death, battered it with all the Ordnance in the Town, and the next day took it: all he found could bear Arms, he put to the Sword, and set their Heads upon Stakes round about the Walls, in the same manner they had used the *Christians,* when they took it. *Moyses* having repaired the Rampires, and thrown down the Work in his Camp, he put in it a strong Garrison, though the pillage he had gotten in the Town was much, having been for a long time an impregnable den of Thieves; yet the loss of the Army so intermingled the sowre with the sweet, as forced *Moyses* to seek a farther revenge, that he sacked *Veratio, Solmos,* and *Kupronka,* and with two thousand Prisoners, most Women and Children, came to *Esenberg,* not far from the Princes Palace, where he there Encamped.

{MN} Regal *assaulted and taken.*

Sigismundus coming to view his Army, was presented with the Prisoners, and six and thirty Ensigns; where celebrating thanks to Almighty God in triumph of those Victories, he was made acquainted with the service *Smith* had done at *Olumpagh, Stoll-Weissenburgh* and *Regal;* for which, with great honour, he gave him three *Turks* Heads in a Shield for his Arms, by Patent, under his Hand and Seal, with an Oath ever to wear them in his Colours, his Picture in Gold, and three hundred Ducats yearly for a Pension.

SIGISMUNDUS BATHORI, *Dei Gratia, Dux* Transilvaniæ, Wallachiæ, & Vandalorum; *Comes* Anchard, Salford, Growenda; *Cunctis his literis significamus qui cas lecturi aut audituri sunt, concessam licentiam aut facultatem* Johanni Smith, *natione* Anglo *Generoso*, 250. *militum Capitaneo sub Illustrissani & Gravissani* Henrici Volda, *Comitis de* Meldri, Salmariæ, & Peldoix *primario, ex* 1000 *equitibus* & 1500. peditibus bello *Ungarico* conductione in Provincias supra scriptas sub Authoritate nostra: cui servituti omni laude, perpetuaq; memoria dignum præbuit sese erga nos, ut virum strenuum pugnantem pro aris & focis decet. Quare e favore nostro militario ipsum ordine condonavimus, & in Sigillum illius tria *Turcica* Capita defignare & deprimere concessimus, que ipso gladio suo ad Urbem *Regalem* in singulari prælio vicit, mactavit, atq; decollavit in *Transilvaniæ* Provincia: Sed fortuna cum variabilis ancepsq; sit idem forte fortuito in *Wallachiæ* Provincia, Anno Domini *1602.* die Mensis Novemberis *18.* cum multis aliis etiam Nubilibus & aliis quibusdam militibus captus est a

Domino *Bascha* electo ex *Cambia* regionis *Tartariæ*, onjus severitate adductus salutum quantem potuit quæsivit, tantumque effecit, Deo omnipotente adjuvante, ut deliberavit se, & ad suos Commilitones revertit; ex quibus ipsum liberavimus, & hæc nobis restimonia habuit ut majori licentia frucretur qua dignus esset, jam tendet in patriam suam dulcissonam: Rogamus ergo omnes nostros charissunos, confinititmos, Duces, Principes, Comites, Barones, Gubernatores Urbium & Navium in cadem Regione & cæterarum Provinciarum in quibus ille refidere conatus fuerit ut idem permittatur Capitaneus libere sine obstaculo omni versari. Hæc facientes pergratum nobis feceritis. Signatum *Lesprizia* in *Misnia* die Mensis *Decembris* 9. *Anno Domini* 1603.

Cum Privilegio propriæ, Majestatis. SIGISMUNDUS BATHORI.

Universis, & singulis, cujuscunq; loci, status, gradut, ordinis, ac conditighis ad quos hos præsens scriptum pervenerit, *Gulielmus Segar, Eques auratus alias dictus Garterus Principalis Rex Armorum* Anglicorum, Salutum. *Sciatis,* quod Ego prædictus Garterus, notum, testatumque facio, quod Patentitem suprascriptum, cum manu propria prædicti Ducis *Transilvaniæ* Subsignatum, & Sigillo suo affixum, Vidi: & Copiam veram ejusdem (in perpetuam rei memoriam) transcripsi, & recordavi in Archivis, & Registris Officii Armorum. Datum *Londini 19.* die Augusti, Anno Domini *1625.* Annoque Regni Domini nostri *CAROLI* Dei gratia Magnæ Britanniæ, Franciæ, & *Hibernix* Regis, Fidei Defendoris, &c. Prime.

GULIELMUS SEGAR, Garterus.

{MN} SIGISMUNDUS BATHORI, by the Grace of God, Duke of *Transilvania, Wallachia,* and *Moldavia,* Earl of *Anchard, Salford* and *Growenda;* to whom this Writing may come or appear. Know that We have given Leave and Licence to *John Smith* an *English Gentleman,* Captain of 250 Soldiers, under the most Generous and Honourable *Henry Volda,* Earl of *Meldritch, Salmaria,* and *Peldoia,* Colonel of a thousand Horse, and fifteen hundred Foot, in the Wars of *Hungary,* and in the Provinces aforesaid under our Authority; whose Service doth deserve all praise, and perpetual Memory towards us, as a Man that did for God and his Country overcome his Enemies; Wherefore out of our Love and Favour, according to the Law of Arms, We have ordained, and given him in his Shield of Arms, the Figure and Description of three Turks Heads, which with his Sword before the Town of *Regal,* in single Combat he did overcome, kill, and cut off, in the Province of *Transilvania.* But Fortune, as she is very variable, so it chanced and happened to him in the Province of *Wallatchia,* in the year of Our Lord 1602. the 18th day of *November,* with many others, as well Noble Men as also divers other Soldiers, were taken Prisoners by the Lord *Bashaw* of *Cambia,* a Country of *Tartaria;* whose cruelty brought him such good Fortune, by the Help and Power of Almighty God, that he delivered himself, and returned again to his Company and fellow Soldiers, of whom We do discharge him, and this he hath in Witness thereof, being much more worthy of a better Reward; and now intends to return to his own sweet Country. We desire therefore all Our loving and kind Kinsmen, Dukes, Princes, Earls, Barons, Governours of Towns, Cities or Ships, in this Kingdom, or any other Provinces he shall come in, that you freely let pass this the aforesaid Captain, without any hindrance or molestation, and this doing, with all kindness, we are always ready to do the like for you. Sealed at *Lipswick* in *Misenland,* the ninth of *December,* in the year of our Lord, 1603.

{MN} *The same in* English.

With the proper privilege of his Majesty. SIGISMUNDUS BATHORI

To all and singular, in what Place, State, Degree, Order, or Condition whatsoever, to whom this present Writing shall come: I *William Segar,* Knight, otherwise Garter, and principal King of Arms of *England,* wish health. Know, that I the aforesaid Garter, do witness and approve, that this aforesaid Patent, I have seen, Signed, and Sealed, under the proper Hand and Seal Manuel of the said Duke of *Transilvania,* and a true Copy of the same, as a thing for perpetual memory, I have Subscribed and Recorded in the Register, and Office of the Heralds of Arms. Dated at *London,* the nineteenth day of *August,* in the year of Our Lord, 1625, and in the first year of our Sovereign Lord *Charles,* by the Grace of God, King of great *Britain, France,* and *Ireland,* Defender of the Faith, &c.

WILLIAM SEGAR.

CHAPTER. IX.

Sigismundus *sends Ambassadours unto the Emperour. The Conditions reassured. He yieldeth up all to* Busca, *and returneth to* Prague.

BUSCA having all this time been raising new Forces, was commanded from the Emperour again to invade *Transilvania*, which being one of the fruitfullest and strongest Countries in those Parts, was now rather a Desart, or the very Spectacle of Desolation; their Fruits and Fields overgrown with Weeds, their Churches and battered Palaces, and best Buildings, as for fear, hid with Moss and Ivy; being the very Bulwark and Rampire of a great part of *Europe*, most fit by all *Christians* to have been supplied and maintained, was thus brought to ruin by them, it most concerned to support it. But alas, what is it, when the Power of Majesty pampered in all delights of pleasant Vanity, neither knowing, nor considering the labour of the Plough-man, the hazard of the Merchant, the oppression of Statesmen, nor feeling the piercing Torments of broken Limbs, and inveterate Wounds, the toilsome Marches, the bad Lodging, the hungry Diet, and the extream misery that Soldiers endure to secure all those Estates, and yet by the spight of malicious detraction, starves for want of their Reward and Recompences, whilst the politique Courtier, that commonly aims more at his own Honours and Ends, than his Countries good, or his Princes Glory, Honour, or Security, as this worthy Prince too well could testifie. But the Emperor being certified how weak and desperate his Estate was, sent *Busca* again with a great Army, to try his fortune once more in *Transilvania*. The Prince considering how his Country and Subjects were consumed, the small means he had any longer to defend his Estate, both against the cruelty of the *Turk*, and the power of the Emperor, and the small care the *Polanders* had in Supplying him, as they had promised, sent to *Busca* to have truce, till Messengers might be sent to the Emperour for some better agreement, wherewith *Busca* was contented. The Ambassadors so prevailed, that the Emperour re-assured unto them the conditions he had promised the Prince at their confederacy for the Lands in *Silesia*, with 60000 Ducats presently in hand, and 50000 Ducats yearly as a Pension. When this conclusion was known to *Moyses*, his Lieutenant then in the Field with the Army, that would do any thing, rather than come in subjection to the *Germans*, he encouraged his Soldiers, and without any more ado, marched to encounter *Busca*, {MN} whom he found much better provided than he expected; so that betwixt them, in six or seven hours, more than five or six thousand, on both sides, lay dead in the field. *Moyses* thus overthrown, fled to the *Turks* at *Temesware*, and his Scattered Troops, some one way, some another.

{MN} *Busca* in *Transilvania* overthroweth *Moyses*.

The Prince understanding of this so sudden and unexpected Accident, only accompanied with an hundred of his Gentry and Nobility, went into the Camp to *Busca*, to let him know how ignorant he was of his Lieutenants error, that he had done it without his direction or knowledge, freely offering to perform what was concluded by his Ambassadors with the Emperor; {MN} and so causing all his Garrisons to come out of their strong Holds, he delivered all to *Busca* for the Emperor, and so went to *Prague*, where he was honourably received, and established in his Possessions, as his Imperial Majesty had promised. *Busca* assembling all the Nobility, took their Oaths of Allegiance and Fidelity, and thus their Prince being gone *Transilvania* became again subject to the Emperor.

{MN} *Sigismundis* yieldeth his country to *Busca*.

{MN} Now after the Death of *Michael*, Vavoid of *Wallachia*, the *Turk* Sent one *Jeremy* to be their Vavoid or Prince; whose insulting Tyranny caused the People to take Arms against him, so that he was forced to flie into the Confines of *Moldavia;* and *Busca* in the behalf of the Emperor, proclaimed the Lord *Rodol* in his stead. But *Jeremy* having assembled an Army of forty thousand *Turks, Tartars,* and *Moldavians,* returned into *Wallachia. Rodol* not yet able to raise such a power, fled into *Transilvania* to *Busca*, his ancient Friend; who considering well of the matter, and how good it would be for his own Security, to have *Wallachia* subject to the Emperor, or at least such an Employment for the remainders of the old Regiments of *Sigismundus,* (of whose Greatness and true Affection he was very suspicious) sent them with *Rodol* to recover *Wallachia,* conducted by the Valiant Captains, the Earl *Meldritch,* Earl *Veltus,* Earl *Nederspolt,* Earl *Zarvana,* the Lord *Becklefield* the Lord *Budendorfe,* with their Regiments, and divers others of great rank and quality, the greatest Friends and Alliances the Prince had; who with Thirty thousand, marched along by the River *Altus,* to the Streights of *Rebrink,* where they entred *Wallachia,* encamping at *Raza; Jeremy* lying at *Argish,* drew his Army into his old Camp, in the Plains of *Peteske,* and with his best diligence fortified it, intending to defend himself, till more power came to him from the *Crim-Tartar.* Many small Parties that came to his Camp, *Rodol* cut off, and in the nights would cause their Heads to be thrown up and down before the Trenches. Seven of their Porters were taken, whom *Jeremy* commanded to be flayed quick, and after hung their Skins upon Poles, and their Carcases and Heads on Stakes by them.

{MN} *Busca* assisteth *Rodol* in *Wallachia*.

CHAPTER. X.

The Battle of Rottenton; a pretty Stratagem of Fire-works by Smith.

RODOL not knowing how to draw the Enemy to Battel, raised his Army, burning and spoiling all where he came, and returned again towards *Rebrink* in the night, as if he had fled upon the general rumour of the *Crim-Tartars* coming, which so inflamed the *Turks* of a happy Victory, they urged *Jeremy* against his Will to follow them. *Rodol* seeing his Plot fell out as he desired, so ordered the matter, that having regained the Streights, he put his Army in order, that had been near two days pursued with continual Skirmishes in his Rear, {MN-1} which now making Head against the Enemy, that followed with their whole Army in the best manner they could, was furiously charged with six thousand *Heydukes*, *Wallachians*, and *Moldavians*, led by three Colonels, *Oversall*, *Dubras*, and *Calab*, to entertain the time till the rest came up; *Veltus* and *Nederspolt* with their Regiments, entertained them with the like courage, till the Zanzacke *Hamesbeg*, with six thousand more, came with a fresh charge, which *Meldritch* and *Budendorfe*, rather like enraged Lions, than Men, so bravely encountred, as if in them only had consisted the Victory; *Meldritch's* Horse being slain under him, the *Turks* pressed what they could to have taken him Prisoner, but being remounted, it was thought with his own hand he slew the valiant Zanzacke, whereupon his Troops retiring, the two proud *Bashawes*, *Aladin*, and *Zizimmus*, brought up the front of the body of their Battle. *Veltus*, and *Nederspolt* having breathed, and joyning their Troops with *Becklefield* and *Zarvana*, with such an incredible courage, charged the left flank of *Zizimmus*, as put them all in disorder, where *Zizimmus* the *Bashaw* was taken Prisoner, but died presently upon his Wounds. *Jeremy* seeing now the main Battel of *Rodol* advance, being thus constrained, like a Valiant Prince in his front of the Vangard, by his example so bravely encouraged his Soldiers, that *Rodol* found no great assurance of the Victory. Thus being joyned in this bloody Massacre, that there was Scarce Ground to stand upon, but upon the dead Carcases, which in less than an hour, were So mingled, as if each Regiment had singled out other. The admired *Aladin* that day did leave behind him a glorious name for his Valour, whose Death, many of his Enemies did lament after the Victory, which at that instant fell to *Rodol*. It was reported, *Jeremy* was also slain; but it Was not so, but fled with the remainder of his Army to *Moldavia*, leaving five and twenty thousand dead in the Field, of both Armies. {MN-2} And thus *Rodol* was seated again in his Soveraignty, and *Wallachia* became subject to the Emperour.

{MN-1} A battle betwixt *Rodol* and *Jeremy*.

{MN-2} *Wallachia* subjected to the Emperour.

But long he rested not to settle his new Estate, but there came News, that certain Regiments of stragling *Tartars*, were foraging those Parts towards *Moldavia*. *Meldritch* with thirteen thousand Men was sent against them, but when they heard it was the *Crim-Tartar*, and his two Sons, with an Army of thirty thousand; and *Jeremy*, that had escaped with fourteen or fifteen thousand, lay in ambush for them about *Langanaw*, he retired towards *Rottenton*, a strong Garrison for *Rodol;* but they were so invironed with these hellish numbers, they could make no great hast for skirmishing with their Scouts, Foragers, and small Parties that still encountred them. But one night amongst the rest, having made a passage through a Wood, with an incredible expedition, cutting Trees thwart each other to hinder their passage, in a thick Fogg, early in the Morning, unexpectedly they met two thousand loaded with Pillage, and two or three hundred Horse and Cattel; the most of them were slain and taken Prisoners, who told them where *Jeremy* lay in the passage, expecting the *Crim-Tartar* that was not far from him. *Meldritch* intending to make his passage by force, was advised of a pretty Stratagem, by the English *Smith*, which presently he thus accomplished; for having accommodated two or three hundred Trunks with wild-fire, upon the Heads of Lances, and charging the Enemy in the night, gave fire to the Trunks, which blazed forth such Flames and Sparkles, that it so amazed not only their Horses, but their Foot also; that by the means of this flaming Encounter, their own Horses turned Tails with such fury, as by their violence overthrew *Jeremy* and his Army, without any loss at all to speak of to *Meldritch*. But of this Victory, long they triumphed not; for being within three Leagues of *Rottenton*, the *Tartar*, with near forty thousand so beset them, that they must either fight, or be cut in pieces flying. Here *Busca*, and the Emperour had their desire; for the Sun no sooner displayed his Beams, than the *Tartar* his Colours; where at mid-day he stayed a while, to see the Passage of a tyrannical and treacherous imposture, till the Earth did blush with the blood of Honesty, that the Sun for shame did hide himself, from so monstrous sight of a cowardly Calamity. It was a most brave sight to see the Banners and Ensigns streaming in the Air, the glittering of Armour, the variety of Colours, the motion of Plumes, the forests of Lances, and the thickness of shorter Weapons, till the silent Expedition of the bloody blast from the murdering Ordnance, whose roaring Voice is not so soon heard, as felt by the aimed at Object, which made among them a most lamentable slaughter.

CHAPTER. XI.

The names of the English *that were slain in the Battel of* Rottenton; *and how Captain* Smith *was taken Prisoner, and sold for a Slave.*

IN THE VALLEY of *Veristhorne,* betwixt the River of *Altus,* and the Mountain of *Rottenton,* was this bloody Encounter, where the most of the dearest Friends of the noble Prince Sigismundus perished. *Meldritch* having ordered his Eleven thousand in the best manner he could, at the Foot of the Mountain upon his Flanks, and before his front, he had pitched sharp Stakes, their Heads hardned in the fire, and bent against the Enemy, as three Battalion of Pikes, amongst the which also, there was digged many small holes. {MN-1} Amongst those Stakes was ranged his foot-men, that upon the charge was to retire, as there was occasion. The *Tartar* having ordered his 40000 for his best advantage, appointed *Mustapha Bashaw* to begin the Battel, with a general Shout, all their Ensigns displaying, Drums beating, Trumpets and Haut-boys sounding. *Nederspolt* and *Mavazo* with their Regiments of Horse most valiantly encountred, and forced them to retire; the *Tartar Begoli* with his Squadrons, darkning the Skies with their flights of numberless Arrows, who was as bravely encountred by *Veltus* and *Oberwin,* which bloody slaughter continued more than an hour, till the matchless multitude of the *Tartars* so increased, that they retired within their Squadrons of Stakes, as was directed. The bloody *Tartar,* as scorning he should stay so long for the Victory, with his massie Troops prosecuted the Charge: But it was a wonder to see how Horse and Man came to the Ground among the Stakes, whose disordered Troops were there so mangled, that the *Christians* with a loud Shout cried *Victoria;* and with five or six field Pieces, planted upon the rising of the Mountain, did much hurt to the Enemy that still continued the Battel with that fury, that *Meldritch* seeing there was no possibility long to prevail, joyned his small Troops in one body, resolved directly to make his passage, or die in the conclusion; and thus in gross gave a general charge, and for more than half an hour, made his way plain before him, till the main Battle of the *Crim-Tartar,* with two Regiments of *Turks* and *Jaizaries* so overmatched them, that they were overthrown. The night approaching, the Earl with some thirteen or fourteen hundred Horse, swam the River, some were drowned, all the rest slain or taken Prisoners: And thus in this bloody Field, near 30000 lay, some Headless, Armless and Legless, all cut and mangled; where breathing their last, they gave this knowledge to the World, that for the lives of so few, the *Crim-Tartar* never paid dearer. {MN-2} But now the Countries of *Transilvania* and *Wallachia* (subjected to the Emperor) and *Sigismundus,* that brave Prince, his Subject and Pensioner, the most of his Nobility, brave Captains and Soldiers, became a prey to the cruel devouring *Turk:* where, had the Emperour been as ready to have assisted him, and those three Armies led by three such worthy Captains, as *Michael, Busca,* and Himself, and had those three Armies joyned together against the *Turk,* let all Men judge, how happy it might have been for all Christendom: and have either regained *Bulgaria,* or at least have beat him out of *Hungaria,* where he hath taken much more from the Emperour, than hath the Emperour from *Transilvania.*

{MN-1} *the Battle of* Rottenton.

{MN-2} *Extracted out of a book, instituted, the Wars of* Hungaria, Wallachia, *and* Moldavia, *written by* Francisco Ferneza, *a learned Italian, the Princes Secretary, and translated by Mr.* Purchas.

In this dismal Battel, where *Nederspolt, Veltus, Zarvana, Mavazo, Bavel,* and many other Earls, Barons, Colonels, Captains, brave Gentlemen, and Soldiers were slain, give me leave to remember the names of our own Country-men, {MN} with him in those Exploits, that as resolutely as the best in the defence of Christ and his Gospel, ended their days, as *Bakersfield, Hardwick, Thomas Milemer, Robert Mollineux, Thomas Bishop, Francis Compton, George Davison, Nicholas Williams* and one *John* a Scot, did what Men could do, and when they could do no more, left there their Bodies in Testimony of their minds; only Ensign *Charleton,* and Sergeant *Robinson* escaped: But *Smith,* among the slaughtered dead Bodies, and many a gasping Soul, with toil and Wounds lay groaning among the rest, till being found by the Pillagers, he was able to live, and perceiving by his Armour and Habit, his ransom might be better to them than his Death, they led him Prisoner with many others; well they used him till his Wounds were cured, and at *Axopolis* they were all sold for Slaves, like Beasts in a Market-place, where every Merchant, viewing their Limbs and Wounds, caused other Slaves to struggle with them, to try their strength, he fell to the share of *Bashaw Bogal,* who sent him forthwith to *Adrianopolis,* so for *Constantinople* to his fair Mistriss for a Slave. By twenty and twenty chained by the Necks, they marched in file to this great City, where they were delivered to their several Masters, and he to the young *Charaza Tragabigzanda.*

{MN} *The English Men in this Battel.*

CHAPTER. XII.

How Captain Smith *was sent Prisoner thorow the* Black *and* Dissabacca *Sea in* Tartaria; *the Description of those seas, and his usage.*

THIS NOBLE Gentlewoman took sometime occasion to shew him to some Friends, or rather to speak with him, because she could speak Italian, would feign her self sick when she should go to the *Bannians,* or weep over the Graves, to know how *Bogal* took him Prisoner; and if he were as the *Bashaw* writ to her, a *Bohemian* Lord conquered by his Hand, as he had many others, which ere long he would present her, whose Ransomes should adorn her with the glory of his Conquests.

But when she heard him protest he knew no such matter, nor ever saw *Bogal,* till he bought him at *Axopolis,* and that he was an *English-man,* only by his Adventures made a Captain in those Countries. To try the truth, she found means to find out many who could speak *English, French, Dutch,* and *Italian,* to whom relating most part of these former Passages she thought necessary, which they so honestly reported to her, she took (as it seemed) much compassion on him; but having no use for him, lest her Mother should sell him, she sent him to her Brother, the *Timor Bashaw* of *Nalbrits,* In the Country of *Cambia,* a Province in *Tartaria.*

{MN-1} Here now let us remember his passing, in this speculative course from *Constantinople* by *Sander, Screw, Panassa, Musa, Lastilla,* to *Varna,* an ancient City upon the *Black Sea.* In all which Journey, having little more liberty, than his eyes judgment, since his Captivity, he might see the Towns with their short Towers, and a most plain, fertile, and delicate Country, especially that most admired place of *Greece,* now called *Romania,* but from *Varna,* nothing but the *Black Sea* Water, till he came to the two Capes of *Taur* and *Pergilos,* where he passed the Streight of *Niger,* which (as he conjectured) is some ten Leagues long, and three broad, betwixt two Low-lands, the Channel is deep, {MN-2} but at the entrance of the Sea *Dissabacca,* there are many great Osie-shaulds, and many great black Rocks, which the *Turks* said were Trees, Weeds, and Mud, thrown from the In-land Countries, by the Inundations and violence of the Current, and cast there by the Eddy. They Sailed by many low Isles, and saw many more of those muddy Rocks, and nothing else, but salt Water, till they came betwixt *Sufax* and *Curuske,* only two white Towns at the entrance of the River *Bruapo* appeared: In six or seven days Sail, he saw four or five seeming strong Castles of Stone, with flat tops and Battlements about them, but arriving at *Cambia,* he was (according to their custom) well used. The River was there more than half a Mile broad. The Castle was of a large Circumference, fourteen or fifteen foot thick, in the

Foundation some six foot from the Wall, is a *Pallizado*, and then a Ditch of about forty foot broad full of Water. On the West side of it, is a Town, all of low flat Houses, which as he conceived, could be of no great strength, yet it keeps all them barbarous Countreys about it in admiration and subjection. After he had stayed there three days; it was two days more before his Guides brought him to *Nalbrits*, where the *Tymor* was then resident, in a great vast Stone Castle, with many great Courts about it, invironed with high Stone Walls, where was quartered their Arms, when they first subjected those Countries, which only live to labour for those Tyrannical *Turks*.

{MN-1} *How he was sent into* Tartaria.

{MN-2} *The Description of the* Dissabacca *Sea*.

{MN} To her unkind Brother, this kind Lady writ so much for his good usage, that he half expected, as much as she intended; for she told him, he should there but sojourn to learn the Language, and what it was to be a *Turk*, till time made her Master of her self. But the *Tymor*, her Brother, diverted all this to the worst of Cruelty; for within an hour after his arrival, he caused his *Drubman* to strip him naked, and shave his Head and Beard so bare as his Hand, a great Ring of Iron, with a long stalk bowed like a Sickle, revitted about his Neck, and a Coat made of *Ulgries* Hair, guarded about with a piece of an undrest Skin. There were many more Christian Slaves, and near an hundred *Forsados* of *Turks* and *Moors*, and he being the last, was slave of Slaves to them all. Among these slavish Fortunes, there was no great choice; for the best was so bad, a Dog could hardly have lived to endure, and yet for all their pains and labours, no more regarded than a Beast.

{MN} Smith's *usage in* Tartaria.

CHAPTER. XIII.

The Turks *diet; the Slaves diet; the attire of the* Tartars; *and manner of Wars and Religions, &c.*

{MN-1} THE *TYMOR* and his Friends fed upon Pillaw, which is, boiled Rice and Garnances with little bits of Mutton or Buckones, which is Roasted pieces of Horse, Bull, Ulgrie, or any Beasts. Samboyses and Muselbit are great Dainties, and yet but round Pies, full of all sorts of Flesh, they can get chopped with variety of Herbs. Their best Drink is Coffee, of a grain they call *Coava*, boiled with Water; and *Sherbeck*, which is only Honey and Water; Mares Milk, or the Milk of any Beast, they hold restorative: but all the Commonalty drink pure Water. {MN-2} Their Bread is made of this *Coava*, which is a kind of black Wheat, and Cuskus a small white Seed, like *Millia* in *Biskay:* But our common Victuals, the entrails of Horse and Ulgries; of this cut in small pieces, they will fill a great Cauldron, and being boiled with *Cuskus,* and put in great Bowls in the form of Chaffing-dishes, they sit round about it on the Ground, after they have raked it thorow, so oft as they please with their foul Fists, the remainder was for the *Christian* Slaves. Some of this Broth, they would temper with *Cuskus* pounded, and putting the Fire off from the Hearth, pour there a Bowl full, then cover it with Coals till it be baked, which stewed with the remainder of the Broth, and some small pieces of Flesh, was an extraordinary Dainty.

{MN-1} *The* Tymor's *Diet of* Cambia, *is as the* Turks.

{MN-2} *The Slaves Diet.*

{MN} The better sort are attired like *Turks,* but the plain *Tartar* hath a black Sheeps-skin over his back, and two of the Legs tied about his Neck; the other two about his middle, with another over his Belly, and the Legs tied in like manner behind him: Then two more, made like a pair of Bases, serveth him for Breeches; with a little close Cap to his Skull of black Felt, and they use exceeding much of this Felt for Carpets, for Bedding, for Coats, and Idols. Their Houses are much worse than your *Irish,* but the In-land Countries have none but Carts and Tents, which they ever remove from Countrey to Countrey, as they see occasion, driving with them infinite Troops of black Sheep, Cattel and Ulgries, eating all up before them as they go.

{MN} *The attire of those* Tartars.

{MN} For the *Tartars* of *Nagi,* they have neither Town, nor House, Corn, nor Drink, but Flesh and Milk. The Milk they keep in great Skins like *Burracho's,* which though it be never so sower, it agreeth well with their strong Stomachs. They live all in *Hordias,* as doth the *Crim-Tartars,* three or four hundred in a Company, in great Carts fifteen or sixteen foot broad, which are covered with small Rods, wattled together in the form of a Bird's Nest, turned upwards, and with the Ashes of Bones, temper'd with Oil, Camels Hair, and a Clay they have, they loam them so well, that no Weather can pierce them, and yet very light. Each *Hordia* hath a *Murse,* which they obey as their King. Their Gods are infinite. One or two thousand of those glittering white Carts drawn with Camels, Deer, Bulls, and Ulgries, they bring round in a Ring, where they pitch their Camp; and the *Murse,* with his chief Alliances, are placed in the midst. They do much hurt, when they can get any *Stroggs,* which are great Boats used up on the River *Volga,* (which they call *Edle*) to them that dwell in the Countrey of *Perolog,* and would do much more, were it not for the *Muscovites* Garrisons that there Inhabit.

{MN} *The* Tartars *of* Nagi *and their manners.*

CHAPTER. XIIII.

The Description of the Crim-Tartars; *their Houses and Carts, their Idolatry in their Lodgings*

{MN-1} NOW YOU are to understand, *Tartary* and *Scythia* are all one, but so large and spacious, few, or none, could ever perfectly describe it, nor all the several kinds of those most barbarous People that inhabit it. Those we call the *Crim-Tartars,* border upon *Moldavia, Podolia, Lithuania,* and *Russia,* are much more regular than the interior parts of *Scythia*. This Great *Tartarian* Prince, that hath so troubled all his Neighbours, they always call *Chan,* which signifieth Emperour; but we, the *Crim-Tartar.* He liveth for the most part in the best Champion Plains of many Provinces; and his removing Court is like a great City of Houses and Tents, drawn on Carts, all so orderly placed East and West, on the right and left hand of the Prince's House, which is always in the midst towards the South, before which, none may pitch their Houses, every one knowing their Order and Quarter, as in an Army. {MN-2} The Princes Houses are very artificially wrought, both the Foundation, Sides, and Roof of Wickers, ascending round to the top like a Dove coat; this they cover with white Salt, or white Earth, temper'd with the Powder of Bones, that it may shine the whiter; sometimes with black Felt, curiously painted with Vines, Trees, Birds, and Beasts; the breadth of the Carts are eighteen or twenty Foot, but the house stretcheth four or five Foot over each side, and is drawn with ten or twelve, or for more state, twenty Camels and Oxen. {MN-3} They have also great Baskets, made of smaller Wickers, like great Chests, with a covering of the same, all covered over with black Felt, rubbed over with Tallow and Sheep's Milk, to keep out the Rain; prettily bedecked with Painting or Feathers; in those they put their Houshold Stuff and Treasure, drawn upon other Carts for that purpose. When they take down their Houses, they set the door always towards the South, and their Carts thirty or forty Foot distant on each side, East and West, as if they were two Walls: The Women also have most curious Carts; every one of his Wives hath a great one for her self, and so many other for her Attendants, that they seem as many Courts as he hath Wives. One great *Tartar* or Nobleman, will have for his particular, more than an hundred of those Houses and Carts, for his several Offices and Uses, but set so far from each other, they will seem like a great Village. {MN-4} Having taken their Houses from the Carts, they place the Master always towards the North; over whose head is always an Image like a Puppet, made of Felt, which they call his Brother; the Women on his left hand, and over the chief Mistriss her Head, such another Brother, and between them a little one, which is the keeper of the House; at the good Wives Beds-feet is a Kids Skin, stuffed with Wooll, and near it a Puppet looking towards the Maids; next the door another, with a dried Cows Udder, for the Women that Milk the Kine, because only the Men Milk Mares; {MN-5} every Morning those Images in their orders, they besprinkle with that they drink, be it Cossmos, or whatsoever, but all the white Mares Milk is reserved for the Prince. Then without the door, thrice to the South, every one bowing his knee in honour of the Fire; then the like to the East, in honour of the Air; then to the West, in honour of the Water; and lastly to the North, in behalf of the dead. After the Servant hath done this duty to the four quarters of the World, he returns into the House, where his Fellows stand waiting, ready with two Cups, and two Basons, to give their Master, and his Wife that lay with him that Night, to wash and drink, who must keep him company all the day following, and all his other Wives come thither to drink, where he keeps his House that day; and all the Gifts presented him till night, are laid up in her Chests; and at the door a Bench full of Cups, and drink for any of them to make merry.

{MN-1} *The description of the* Crim-Tartar's *Court.*

{MN-2} *His Houses and Carts.*

{MN-3} *Baskets.*

{MN-4} *Their Idolatry in their Lodgings.*

{MN-5} *Cosmos is Mares Milk.*

CHAPTER. XV.

Their Feasts, common Diet, Princes Estate, Buildings, Tributes, Laws, Slaves, Entertainment of Ambassadors.

{MN} FOR THEIR FEASTS, they have all sorts of Beasts, Birds, Fish, Fruits, and Herbs they can get, but the more variety of wild ones is the best; to which they have excellent Drink made of Rice, Millet, and Honey, like Wine; they have also Wine, but in Summer they drink most Cossmos, that standeth ready always at the entrance of the door, and by it a Fidler; when the Master of the House beginneth to drink, they all cry, ha, ha, and the Fidler plays, then they all clap their Hands and dance, the Men before their Masters, the Women before their Mistresses; and ever when he drinks, they cry as before; then the Fidler stayeth till they drink all round; sometimes they will drink for the Victory; and to provoke one to drink, they will pull him by the Ears, and lug and draw him, to stretch and beat him, clapping their Hands, stamping with their Feet, and dancing before the Champions, offering them Cups, then draw them back again to increase their Appetite; and thus continue till they be drunk, or their drink done, which they hold an honour, and no Infirmity.

{MN} *Their Feasts.*

{MN} Though the Ground be fertile, they sow little Corn, yet the Gentlemen have Bread and Honey-wine; Grapes they have plenty, and Wine privately, and good Flesh and Fish; but the common sort stamped Millet, mingled with Milk and Water. They call Cassa for Meat, and drink any thing; also any Beast unprofitable for service they kill, when they are like to die, or however they die, they will eat them, Guts, Liver and all; but the most fleshy parts they cut in thin slices, and hang it up in the Sun and Wind without salting, where it will dry so hard, it will not putrifie in a long time. A Ramm they esteem a great Feast among forty or fifty, which they cut in pieces boiled or roasted, puts it in a great Bowl, with Salt and Water, for other Sawce they have none; the Master of the Feast giveth every one a piece, which he eateth by himself, or carrieth away with him. {MN-2} Thus their hard fare makes them so infinite in Cattel, and their great number of Captive Women to breed upon, makes them so populous. But near the Christian Frontiers, the baser sort make little Cottages of Wood, called *Vlusi*, daubed over with dirt, and Beasts dung covered with sedge; yet in Summer they leave them, beginning their Progress in *April,* with their Wives, Children, and Slaves, in their Carted Houses, scarce convenient for four or five Persons; driving their Flocks towards *Precopia,* and sometimes into *Taurica,* or *Osow,* a Town upon the River

Tanais, which is great and swift, where the *Turk* hath a Garrison; and in *October* return again to their Cottages. Their Clothes are the Skins of Dogs, Goats, and Sheep, lined with Cotton Cloath, made of their finest Wooll, for of their worst they make their Felt, which they use in abundance, as well for Shooes and Caps, as Houses, Beds, and Idols; also of the coarse Wooll mingled with Horse hair, they make all their Cordage. {MN-3} Notwithstanding this wandring life, their Princes sit in great State upon Beds, or Carpets, and with great reverence are attended both by Men and Women, and richly served in Plates and great Silver Cups, delivered upon the Knee, attired in rich Furrs, lined with Plush, or Taffity, or Robes of Tissue. These *Tartars* possess many large and goodly Plains, wherein feed innumerable Herds of Horse and Cattel, as well wild as tame; which are Elkes, Bisons, Horses, Deer, Sheep, Goats, Swine, Bears, and divers others.

{MN-1} *Their common diet.*

{MN-2} *How they become populous.*

{MN-3} *Their Princes State.*

{MN-1} In those Countries are the Ruins of many fair Monasteries, Castles, and Cities, as *Bacasaray, Salutium, Almassary, Precopia, Cremum, Sedacom, Capha,* and divers others by the Sea, but all kept with strong Garrisons for the Great *Turk*, {MN-2} who yearly by Trade or Traffick, receiveth the chief Commodities those fertile Countries afford, as Bezoar, Rice, Furs, Hides, Butter, Salt, Cattel, and Slaves, yet by the spoils they get from the secure and idle Christians, they maintain themselves in this Pomp. Also their Wives, of whom they have as many as they will, very costly, yet in a constant custom with decency.

{MN-1} *Ancient Buildings.*

{MN-2} *Commodities for tribute to the* Turk.

{MN} They are *Mahometans*, as are the *Turks*, from whom they also have their Laws, but no Lawyers, nor Attorneys, only Judges, and Justices in every Village, or Hordia; but Capital Criminals, or matters of moment, before the Chan himself, or Privy Councils, of whom they are always heard, and speedily discharged; for any may have access at any time to them, before whom they appear with great Reverence, adoring their Princes as Gods, and their Spiritual Judges as Saints; for Justice is with such integrity and Expedition Executed, without Covetousness, Bribery, Partiality, and Brawling, that in six Months they have sometimes scarce six Causes to hear. About the Princes

Court, none but his Guard wear any Weapon, but abroad they go very strong, because there are many Bandittos, and Thieves.

{MN} *Good Laws, yet no Lawyers.*

{MN} They use the *Hungarians, Russians, Wallachians,* and *Moldavian* Slaves (whereof they have plenty) as Beasts to every work; and those *Tartars* that serve the Chan, or Noblemen, have only Victuals and Apparel, the rest are generally nasty, and idle, naturally miserable, and in their Wars better Thieves than Soldiers.

{MN} *Their Slaves.*

{MN} This Chan hath yearly a Donative from the King of *Poland,* the Dukes of *Lithuania, Moldavia,* and *Nagayon Tartars;* their Messengers commonly he useth bountifully, and very nobly, but sometimes most cruelly; when any of them do bring their Presents, by his Houshold Officers, they are entertained in a plain Field, with a moderate proportion of Flesh, Bread and Wine, for once; but when they come before him, the *Sultans, Tuians, Vlans, Marhies,* his chief Officers and Councellors attend, one Man only bringeth the Ambassadour to the Court Gate, but to the Chan he is led between two Councellors; where saluting him upon their bended knees, declaring their message, are admitted to eat with him, and presented with a great Silver Cup full of Mead from his own hand, but they drink it upon their Knees: when they are dispatched, he invites them again, the Feast ended, they go back a little from the Palace door, and rewarded with Silk Vestures, wrought with Gold down to their Anckles, with an Horse or two, and sometimes a Slave of their own Nation; in them Robes presently they come to him again, to give him thanks, take their leave, and so depart.

{MN} *His Entertainment of Ambassadours.*

CHAPTER. XVI.

How he levieth an Army; their Arms and Provision; how he divideth the Spoil, and his Service to the Great Turk.

{MN} WHEN HE INTENDS any Wars, he must first have leave of the Great *Turk*, whom he is bound to assist when he commandeth, receiving daily for himself and chief of his Nobility, Pensions from the *Turk*, that holds all Kings but Slaves, that pay Tribute, or are subject to any: signifying his intent to all his Subjects, within a Month commonly he raiseth his Army, and every Man is to furnish himself for three Months Victuals, which is parched Millet, or ground to Meal, which they ordinarily mingle with Water (as is said) hard Cheese or Curds dried, and beaten to powder, a little will make much Water like Milk, and dried Flesh, this they put also up in Sacks; The Chan and his Nobles have some Bread and *Aquavitæ*, and quick Cattel to kill when they please, wherewith very sparingly they are contented. Being provided with expert Guides, and got into the Country he intends to Invade, he sends forth his Scouts to bring in what Prisoners they can, from whom he will wrest the utmost of their Knowledge fit for his purpose; having advised with his Council, what is most fit to be done, the Nobility, according to their Antiquity, doth march; then moves he with his whole Army: if he find there is no Enemy to oppose him, he adviseth how far they shall Invade, commanding every Man (upon pain of his Life) to kill all the obvious Rusticks; but not to hurt any Women, or Children.

{MN} *How he levieth an Army.*

{MN} Ten, or fifteen thousand, he commonly placeth, where he findeth most convenient for his standing Camp; the rest of his Army he divides in several Troops, bearing ten or twelve Miles square before them, and ever within three or four days return to their Camp, putting all to Fire and Sword, but that they carry with them back to their Camp; and in this scattering manner he will invade a Country, and be gone with his Prey, with an incredible Expedition. But if he understand of an Enemy, he will either fight in Ambuscado, or flie; for he will never fight any Battel if he can chuse, but upon treble advantage; yet by his innumerable flights of Arrows, I have seen flie from his flying Troops, we could not well judge, whether his fighting or flying was most dangerous, so good is his Horse, and so expert his Bow-men; but if they be so intangled they must fight, there is none can be more hardy, or resolute in their defences.

{MN} *The manner of his Wars.*

{MN} Regaining his own Borders, he takes the tenth of the principal Captives, Man, Woman, Child, or Beast (but his Captains that take them, will accept of some particular Person they best like for themselves) the rest are divided amongst the whole Army, according to every Mans Desert and Quality; that they keep them, or sell them to who will give most; but they will not forget to use all the means they can, to know their Estates, Friends, and Quality, and the better they find you, the worse they will use you, till you do agree to pay such a Ransom, as they will impose upon you; therefore many great Persons have endured much misery to conceal themselves, because their Ransoms are so intolerable: their best hope is of some Christian Agent, that many times cometh to redeem Slaves, either with Money, or Man for Man; those Agents knowing so well the extream covetousness of the *Tartars*, do use to bribe some Jew or Merchant, that feigning they will sell them again to some other Nation, are oft redeemed for a very small Ransom.

{MN} *How he divideth the spoil.*

{MN} But to this *Tartarian* Army, when the *Turk*, commands, he goeth with some small Artillery; and the *Nagayans, Precopens, Crims, Osovens,* and *Circassians,* are his Tributaries; but the *Perigorves, Oczaconians, Bialogordens,* and *Dobrucen Tartars,* the *Turk* by Covenant commands to follow him, so that from all those *Tartars* he hath had an Army of an hundred and twenty thousand excellent, swift, stomackfull *Tartarian* Horse for foot they have none. Now the Chan, his Sultans and Nobility, use *Turkiso, Caramanian, Arabian, Parthian,* and other strange *Tartarian* Horses; the swiftest they esteem the best; seldom they feed any more at home, than they have present use for; but upon their Plains is a short Wood-like Heath, in some Countries like Gail, full of Berries, much better than any Grass.

{MN} *How the Chan doth serve the Great* Turk.

{MN} Their Arms are such, as they have surprised or got from the *Christians* or *Persians,* both Brest-plates, Swords, Scimitars, and Helmets; Bows and Arrows they make most themselves, also their Bridles and Saddles are indifferent, but the Nobility are very handsome, and well armed like the *Turks,* in whom consisteth their greatest Glory; the ordinary sort have little Armour, some a plain young Pole unshaven, headed with a piece of Iron for a Lance; some an old *Christian* Pike, or a *Turks* Cavarine, yet those Tattertimallions will have two or three Horses, some four or five, as well for service, as for to eat; which makes their Armies seem thrice so many as there are Soldiers. The Chan himself hath about his Person, Ten thousand chosen

Tartars and *Janizaries,* some small Ordnance, and a white Mares Tail, with a piece of green Taffity on a great Pike, is carried before him for a Standard; because they hold no Beast so precious as a white Mare, whose Milk is only for the King and Nobility, and to Sacrifice to their Idols; but the rest have Ensigns of divers Colours.

{MN} *Their Arms.*

For all this miserable Knowledge, Furniture, and Equipage, the mischief they do in *Christendom* is wonderful, by reason of their hardness of Life and Constitution, Obedience, Agility, and their Emperours Bounty, Honours, Grace, and Dignities he ever bestoweth upon those, that have done him any memorable Service in the face of his Enemies.

{MN} The Caspian Sea, most Men agree that have passed it, to be in length about 200 Leagues, and in breadth an hundred and fifty, environed to the East, with the great Desarts of the *Tartars* of *Turkomania;* to the West, by the *Circasses,* and the Mountain *Caucasus;* to the North, by the River *Volga,* and the Land of *Nagay;* and to the South, by *Media,* and *Persia:* This Sea is fresh Water in many places, in others as salt as the great Ocean; it hath many great Rivers which fall into it, as the mighty River of *Volga,* which is like a Sea, running near Two thousand Miles, through many great and large Countries, that send into it many other great Rivers; also out of *Saberia, Yaick,* and *Yem,* out of the great Mountain *Caucasus,* the River *Sirus, Arash,* and divers others, yet no Sea nearer it than the black Sea, which is at least an hundred Leagues distant: In which Country live the *Georgians,* now part *Armenians,* part *Nestorians;* it is neither found to increase or diminish, or empty it self any way, except it be under Ground, and in some places they can find no Ground at Two hundred fathom.

{MN} *A Description of the* Caspian *Sea.*

Many other most strange and wonderful things are in the Land of *Cathay,* towards the North-east, and China towards the South-east, where are many of the most famous Kingdoms in the World, where most Arts, Plenty, and Curiosities are in such abundance, as might seem incredible, which hereafter I will relate, as I have briefly gathered from such Authors as have lived there.

CHAPTER. XVII.

How Captain Smith *escaped his Captivity; slew the* Bashaw *of* Nalbrits *in* Cambia; *his Passage to* Russia, Transilvania, *and the middest of* Europe *to* Africa.

{MN-1} ALL THE HOPE he had ever to be delivered from this Thraldom, was Only the love of *Tragabigzanda*, who surely was ignorant of his bad usage; for although he had often debated the matter with some Christians, that had been there a long time Slaves, they could not find how to make an escape, by any reason or possibility; but God beyond Man's Expectation or Imagination helpeth his Servants, when they least think of help, as it hapned to him. So long he lived in this miserable Estate, as he became a Thresher at a grange in a great Field, more than a League from the *Timor's* House; the *Bashaw*, as he oft used to visit his Granges, visited him, and took occasion so to beat, spurn, and revile him, that forgetting all reason, he beat out the *Timor's* Brains with his Threshing Bat, for they have no Flails; and seeing his Estate could be no worse than it was, clothed himself in his Clothes, hid his Body under the Straw, filled his Knapsack with Corn, shut the doors, mounted his Horse, and ran into the Desart at all adventure; two or three days, thus fearfully wandring he knew not whither, and well it was, he met not any to ask the way; being even as taking leave of this miserable World, {MN-2} God did direct him to the great way or Castragan, as they call it, which doth cross these large Territories, and generally known among them by these marks.

{MN-1} *How* Smith *escaped his Captivity.*

{MN-2} *Their Guides in those Countries.*

In every crossing of this great way is planted a Post, and in it so many bobs with broad ends, as there be ways, and every bob the Figure painted on it, that demonstrateth to what part that way leadeth; as that which pointeth towards the *Crim's* Country, is marked with a half Moon, if towards the *Georgians* and *Persia*, a black Man, full of white spots, if towards *China*, the Picture of the Sun, if towards *Muscovia*, the Sign of a Cross, if towards the Habitation of any other Prince, the Figure whereby his Standard is known. To his dying Spirits thus God added some comfort in this melancholy Journey, wherein if he had met any of that vile Generation, they had made him their Slave, or knowing the Figure Engraven in the Iron about his Neck, (as all Slaves have) he had been sent back again to his Master; sixteen days he travelled in this fear and torment, after the Cross, till he arrived at *Æcopolis*, upon the River *Don*, a Garrison of the *Muscovites*. The Governour after due Examination of those his hard events, took off his Irons, and so kindly used him, he thought himself new risen from the Dead, and the good Lady *Calamata*, largely Supplied all his wants.

{MN-1} This is as much as he could learn of those wild Countries, that the Country of *Cambia* is two days Journey from the Head of the great River *Bruapo*, which springeth from many places of the Mountains of *Innagachi*, that joyn themselves together in the Pool *Kerkas* which they account for the Head, and falleth into the Sea *Dissabacca*, called by some the Lake *Maeotas*, which receiveth also the River *Tanais*, and all the Rivers that fall from the great Countries of the *Circassi*, the *Cartaches*, and many from the *Tauricaes*, *Precopes*, *Cummani*, *Cossunka*, and the *Crim;* through which Sea he Sailed, and up the River *Bruapo* to *Nalbrits*, and thence through the Desarts of *Circassi* to *Æcopolis*, as is related; where he stayed with the Governour, till the Convoy went to *Caragnaw;* then with his Certificate how he found him, and had examined with his friendly Letters, sent him by *Zumalack* to *Caragnaw*, whose Governour in like manner so kindly used him, that by this means he went with a safe conduct to *Lesch*, and *Donko*, in *Cologoske*, and thence to *Berniske*, and *Newgrod* in *Siberia*, by *Rezechica*, upon the River *Nieper*, in the confines of *Lithuania;* from whence with as much kindness, he was convoyed in like manner by *Coroski, Duberesko, Duzihell, Drohobus,* and *Ostroge* in *Volonia; Saslaw*, and *Lasco* in *Podolia; Halico* and *Collonia* in *Polonia;* and so to *Hermonstat* in *Transilvania*. In all this his life, he seldom met with more Respect, Mirth, Content and Entertainment; and not any Governour where he came, but gave him somewhat as a Present, besides his Charges; seeing themselves as subject to the like Calamity. {MN-2} Through those poor continually Foraged Countries, there is no passage, but with the Caravans or Convoys; for they are Countries rather to be pitied than envied; and it is a wonder any should make Wars for them. The Villages are only here and there, a few Houses of streight Firr Trees, laid heads and points above one another, made fast by notches at the ends, more than a Man's heighth, and with broad split Boards, pinned together with woodden Pins, as thatched for coverture. In ten Villages you shall scarce find ten Iron Nails, except it be in some extraordinary Man's House. For their Towns, *Æcopolis*, *Letch*, and *Donko*, have Rampires made of that woodden Walled fashion, double, and betwixt them Earth and Stones, but so latched with cross Timber, they are very strong against any thing but Fire; and about them a deep Ditch, and a Palizado of young Firr Trees; but most of the rest have only a great Ditch cast about them, and the Ditches Earth, is all their Rampire; but round, well environed with Palizadoes. Some have some few small pieces of small Ordnance, and Slings, Calievers, and Muskets, but their generallest Weapons are the *Russe* Bows and Arrows; you shall find Pavements over Bogs, only of young Firr-Trees, laid cross one over another, for two or three hours Journey, or as the Passage requires, and yet in two days Travel, you shall scarce see six Habitations. Notwithstanding to see how their Lords, Governours, and Captains are civilized, well attired and accoutred with Jewels, Sables, and Horses, and after their manner with curious Furniture, it is wonderful; but they are all Lords or Slaves, which makes them so subject to every Invasion.

{MN-1} *The description of* Cambia, *and his passage to* Russia.

{MN-2} *His Observations in his Journey to* Transilvania, *through the midst of* Europe.

In *Transilvania*, he found so many good Friends, that but to see, and rejoyce himself (after all those Encounters) in his Native Country, he would ever hardly have left them, though the mirrour of vertue their Prince was absent. Being thus glutted with content, and near drowned with Joy, he parted high *Hungaria* by *Fileck, Tocka, Cassovia,* and *Underorowoay,* by *Ulmicht* in *Moravia,* to *Prague* in *Bohemia;* at last he found the most gracious Prince *Sigismundus,* with his Colonel at *Lipswick* in *Misenland,* who gave him his Pass, intimating the service he had done, and the Honours he had received, with fifteen hundred Ducats of Gold to repair his Losses: With this he spent some time to visit the fair Cities and Countries of *Dresden* in *Saxony, Magdeburgh* and *Brunswick; Cassel* in *Hessen; Wittenberg, Vilum,* and *Minekin* in *Bavaria; Augsburg,* and her Universities; *Hama, Frankford, Mentz,* the *Palatinate; Worms, Spires,* and *Straburg;* passing *Nancie* in *Lorain,* and *France* by *Paris* to *Orleans,* he went down the River of *Loyer,* to *Angiers,* and imbarked himself at *Nantz* in *Britain,* for *Bilbao* in *Biskay* to see *Burgos-Valladolid,* the admired Monastery of the *Escurial, Madrid, Toledo, Corduba, Cuedyrial, Sivil, Cheries, Cales,* and St. *Lucas* in *Spain.*

CHAPTER. XVIII.

The Observations of Captain Smith; *Mr.* Henry Archer, *and others in* Barbary.

BEING thus satisfied with *Europe* and *Asia,* understanding of the Wars in *Barbary,* he went from *Gibralter* to *Ceuta* and *Tangier,* thence to *Saffee,* where growing into Acquaintance with a French Man of War, the Captain and some twelve more went to *Morocco,* to see the ancient Monuments of that large renowned City: It was once the principal City in *Barbary,* situated in a goodly plain Country, 14 Miles from the great Mount *Atlas,* and sixty Miles from the *Atlantick* Sea; but now little remaining, but the King's Palace, which is like a City of it self; and the Christian Church, on whose flat, {MN-1} square Steeple is a great broach of Iron, whereon is placed the three Golden Balls of Africa: The first is near three Ells in Circumference, the next above it somewhat less, the uppermost the least over them, as it were an half Ball, and over all a pretty gilded Pyramid. Against those Golden Balls hath been shot many a shot, their Weight is recorded 700 weight of pure Gold, hollow within, yet no shot did ever hit them, nor could ever any Conspirator attain that Honour as to get them down. They report, the Prince of *Morocco* betrothed himself to the King's Daughter of *Æthiopia,* he dying before their Marriage, she caused those three Golden Balls to be set up for his Monument, and vowed Virginity all her Life. {MN-2} The *Alfantica* is also a place of note, because it is invironed with a great Wall, wherein lie the Goods of all the Merchants securely guarded. The *Inderea* is also (as it were) a City of it self, where dwell the Jews: The rest for the most part is defaced; but by the many Pinnacles and Towers, with Balls on their tops, hath much appearance of much sumptuousness and curiosity. There have been many famous Universities, which are now but Stables for Fowls, and Beasts, and the Houses in most parts lie tumbled one above another; the Walls of Earth are with the great fresh Floods washed to the ground; nor is there any Village in it, but Tents for Strangers, *Larbes* and *Moors*. Strange Tales they will tell of a great Garden, wherein were all sorts of Birds, Fishes, Beasts, Fruits, and Fountains, which for Beauty, Art and Pleasure, exceeded any place known in the World, though now nothing but Dung-hills, Pigeon-Houses, Shrubs and Bushes. There are yet many excellent Fountains, adorned with Marble, and many Arches, Pillars, Towers, Ports, and Temples; but most only reliques of lamentable Ruins and sad Desolation.

{MN-1} *The three Golden Balls of* Africa.

{MN-2} *The description of* Morocco.

{MN} When *Muly Hamet* Reigned in *Barbary*, he had three Sons, *Muly Sheck, Muly Sidan,* and *Muly Bufferres,* he a most good and noble King, that governed well with Peace and Plenty, till his Empress, more cruel than any Beast in Africa, poisoned him, her own Daughter, *Muly Sheck,* his eldest Son, born of a Portugal Lady, and his Daughter, to bring *Muly Sidan,* to the Crown now reigning, which was the cause of all those brawls, and Wars that followed betwixt those Brothers, their Children, and a Saint that started up, but he played the Devil.

{MN} *A bloody Empress.*

{MN-1} King *Muly Hamet* was not black, as many suppose, but *Molara,* or tawny, as are the most of his Subjects; every way noble, kind and friendly, very rich and pompous in State and Majesty, though he sitteth not upon a Throne nor Chair of state, but cross Leg'd upon a rich Carpet, as doth the *Turk,* whose Religion of *Mahomet,* with an incredible miserable Curiosity they observe. His ordinary Guard is at least 5000, but in Progress, he goeth not with less than 20000 Horse-men, himself as rich in all his Equipage, as any Prince in Christendom, and yet a Contributor to the *Turk.* {MN-2} In all his Kingdom were so few good Artificers, that he entertained from *England,* Gold-smiths, Plummers, Carvers, and Polishers of Stone, and Watch-makers, so much he delighted in the Reformation of Workmanship, he allowed each of them ten Shillings a day standing Fee, Linen, Woollen, Silks, and what they would for Diet and Apparel, and Custom-free to transport, or import what they would; for there were scarce any of those qualities in his Kingdom, but those, of which there are divers of them, living at this present in *London.* Amongst the rest, one Mr. *Henry Archer,* a Watch-maker, walking in *Morocco,* from the *Alfantica* to the *Juderea,* the way being very foul, met a great Priest, or a *Sante* (as they call all great Clergy-men) who would have thrust him into the dirt for the way; but Archer not knowing what he was, gave him a box on the Ear, presently he was apprehended, and condemned to have his Tongue cut out, and his Hand cut off: But no sooner it was known at the King's Court, but 300 of his Guard came, and broke open the Prison, and delivered him although the Fact was next degree to Treason.

{MN-1} *King* Muly Hamet *or the Great* Zeriff *of* Barbary.

{MN-2} *His great love to English Men.*

{MN} Concerning this *Archer,* there is one thing more worth noting: Not far from Mount *Atlas,* a great Lioness in the heat of the day, did use to bathe her self, and teach her young Puppies to swim in the River *Cauzef*, of a good breadth; yet she would carry, which some *Moors* perceiving, watched there them one after another over the River; opportunity, and when the River was between her and them, stole four of her Whelps, which she perceiving, with all the speed she could passed the River, and coming near them, they let fall a Whelp (and fled with the rest) which she took in her mouth, and so returned to the rest: A Male and a Female of those they gave Mr. *Archer*, who kept them in the King's Garden, till the Male killed the Female, then he brought it up as a Puppy-dog lying upon his Bed, till it grew so great as a Mastiff, and no dog more tame or gentle to them he knew: But being to return for *England*, at *Saffee* he gave him to a Merchant of *Marseillses*, that presented him to the French King, who sent him to King James, where it was kept in the Tower seven Years: After one Mr. *John Bull*, then Servant to Mr. *Archer*, with divers of his Friends, went to see the Lions, not knowing any thing at all of him; yet this rare Beast smelled him before he saw him, whining, groaning, and tumbling, with such an expression of acquaintance, that being informed by the Keepers how he came thither; Mr. *Bull* so prevailed, the Keeper opened the Grate, and *Bull* went in: But no Dog could fawn more on his Master, than the Lion on him, licking his Feet, Hands, and Face, skipping and tumbling to and fro, to the wonder of all the beholders; being satisfied with his acquaintance, he made shift to get out of the Grate: But when the Lion saw his Friend gone, no Beast by bellowing, roaring, scratching, and howling, could express more rage and sorrow, nor in four days after would he either eat or drink.

{MN} *The strange love of a Lion.*

{MN} In *Morocco*, the King's Lions are altogether in a Court, invironed with a great high Wall; to those they put a young Puppy-dog: The greatest Lion had a sore upon his neck, which this Dog so licked, that he was healed: The Lion defended him from the fury of all the rest, nor durst they eat till the Dog and he had fed; this Dog grew great, and lived amongst them many years after.

{MN} *Another kind Lion in* Morocco.

{MN-1} *Fez* also is a most large and plentiful Country, the chief City is called *Fez*, divided into two parts; old *Fez*, containing about 80 thousand Households, the other 4000 pleasantly situated upon a River in the heart of *Barbary*, part upon Hills, part upon Plains, full of people, and all sorts of Merchandize. The great Temple is called *Carucen*, in breadth seventeen Arches, in length 120, born up with 2500 white Marble Pillars: under the chief

Arch, where the Tribunal is kept, hangeth a most huge Lamp, compassed with 110 lesser, under the other also hang great Lamps, and about some, are burning fifteen hundred lights, They say, they were all made of the Bells the *Arabians* brought from *Spain*. It hath three Gates of notable heighth, Priests and Officers so many, that the Circuit of the Church, the Yard, and other Houses, is little less than a Mile and half in compass, there are in this City 200 Schools, 200 Inns, 400 Water-Mills, 600 Water-Conduits, 700 Temples and Oratories; but 50 of them most stately and richly furnished. Their *Alcazer* or *Burse* is Walled about, it hath twelve Gates, and fifteen Walks covered with Tents, to keep the Sun from the Merchants, and them that come there. The King's Palace, both for strength and beauty is excellent, and the Citizens have many great Privileges. Those two Countries of *Fez* and *Morocco*, are the best part of all *Barbary*, abounding with People, Cattel, and all good Necessaries for Man's use. For the rest, as the *Larbs*, or Mountainers, the Kingdoms of *Cocow, Algier, Tripoli, Tunis,* and *Ægypt;* there are many large Histories of them in divers Languages, especially that writ by that most excellent Statesman, *John de Leo*, who afterwards turned Christian. {MN-2} The unknown Countries of *Guine* and *Binn*, this six and twenty years have been frequented with a few English Ships only to Trade, especially the River of *Senega*, by Captain *Brimstead*, Captain *Brockit*, Mr. *Crump*, and divers others. Also the great River of *Gambia*, by Captain *Johnson*, who is returned in thither again, in the Year 1626, with Mr. *William Grent*, and thirteen or fourteen others, to stay in the Country, to discover some way to those rich Mines of *Gago* or *Tumbatu*, from whence is supposed the *Moors* of *Barbary* have their Gold, and the certainty of those supposed Descriptions and Relations of those interiour parts, which daily the more they are sought into, the more they are corrected: For surely, those interiour Parts of Africa, are little known to either *English, French,* or *Dutch,* though they use much the Coast; therefore we will make a little bold with the Observations of the *Portugals*.

{MN-1} *The description of* Fez.

{MN-2} *A brief description of the most unknown parts of* Africa.

CHAPTER. XIX.

The strange Discoveries and Observations of the Portugals *in* Africa.

{MN} THE PORTUGALS on those Parts have the glory, who first coasting along this Western Shoar of *Africa*, to find passage to the *East-Indies*, within this hundred and fifty years, even from the Streights of *Gibraltar*, about the Cape of *Bone Esperance* to the *Persian* Gulf, and thence all along the *African* Coast to the *Moluccas*, have subjected many great Kingdoms, erected many Common-wealths, built many great and strong Cities; and where is it they have not been by Trade or Force? No not so much as *Cape de Verd*, and *Sermleone;* but most Bays or Rivers, where there is any Trade to be had, especially Gold, or conveniency for Refreshment, but they are scattered; living so amongst those Blacks, by time and cunning, they seem to be naturalized amongst them. As for the Isles of the *Canaries*, they have fair Towns, many Villages, and many thousands of People rich in Commodities.

{MN} *How the* Portugals *coasted to the* East Indies.

{MN} *Ordoardo Lopez*, a noble *Portuguse, Anno Dom.* 1578, imbarking himself for *Congo* to Trade, where he found such Entertainment, finding the King much oppressed with Enemies, he found means to bring in the *Portugals* to assist him, whereby he planted there Christian Religion, and spent most of his life to bring those Countries to the Crown of *Portugal*, which he describeth in this manner.

{MN} *Or* Edward.

{MN} The Kingdom of *Congo* is about 600 Miles Diameter any way, the chief City called St. *Savadore,* seated upon an exceeding high Mountain, 150 Miles from the Sea, very fertile, and Inhabited with more than 100000 Persons, where is an excellent Prospect over all the plain Countries about it, well watered, lying (as it were) in the Center of this Kingdom, over all which the *Portugals* now command, though but an handful in comparison of *Negroes*. They have Flesh and Fruits very plentiful of divers sorts.

{MN} *The Kingdom of* Congo.

{MN} This Kingdom is divided into five Provinces, viz. *Bamba, Sundi, Pango, Batta* and *Pembo;* but *Bamba* is the Principal, and can afford 400000 Men of War. Elephants are bred over all those Provinces, and of wonderful greatness;

though some report, they cannot kneel, nor lie down, they can do both, and have their Joynts as other Creatures for use: With their Fore-feet they will leap upon Trees to pull down the Boughs, and are of that strength, they will shake a great *Cocao* Tree for the Nuts, and pull down a good Tree with their Tusks, to get the Leaves to eat, as well as Sedge and long Grass, *Cocao* Nuts and Berries, &c. which with their Trunk they put in their Mouth, and chew it with their smaller Teeth; in most of those Provinces, are many rich Mines, but the *Negroes* opposed the *Portugueses* for working in them.

{MN} *Wild Elephants.*

{MN} The Kingdom of *Angola* is wonderful populous, and rich in Mines of Silver, Copper, and most other Metals; fruitfull in all manner of Food, and sundry sorts of Cattel, but Dogs Flesh they love better than any other Meat; they use few Clothes, and no Armour; Bows, Arrows, and Clubs are their Weapons. But the *Portugueses* are well armed against those Engines, and do buy yearly of those Blacks more than five thousand Slaves, and many are People exceeding well proportioned.

{MN} *The Kingdom of* Angola.

{MN-1} The *Anchios* are a most valiant Nation, but most strange to all about them. Their Arms are Bows; short and small, wrapped about with Serpents Skins, of divers Colours, but so smooth, you would think them all one with the Wood, and it makes them very strong; their Strings little twigs, but exceeding tough and flexible; their Arrows short, which they shoot with an incredible quickness. They have short Axes of Brass and Copper for Swords; wonderful, loyal and faithful, and exceeding simple, yet so active, they skip amongst the Rocks like Goats. {MN-2} They trade with them of *Nubea*, and *Congo*, for *Lamach*, which is a small kind of Shell-fish, of an excellent azure, colour, Male and Female, but the Female they hold most pure; they value them at divers prices, because they are of divers sorts, and those they use for Coin, to buy and sell, as we do Gold and Silver; nor will they have any other Money in all those Countries, for which they give Elephants Teeth; and Slaves for Salt, Silk, Linen Cloth, Glass-beads, and such like *Portugal* Commodities.

{MN-1} *The Kingdom of* Anchios.

{MN-2} *A strange Memr'y.*

{MN} They circumcise themselves, and mark their Faces with sundry slashes from their Infancy. They keep a shambles of Man's Flesh, as if it were Beef, or other Victuals; for when they cannot have a good Market for their Slaves; or their Enemies they take, they kill, and sell them in this manner; some are so resolute, in shewing how much they scorn death, they will offer themselves and Slaves, to this Butchery to their Prince and Friends; and though there be many Nations will eat their Enemies, in *America* and *Asia,* yet none but those are known to be so mad, as to eat their Slaves and Friends also.

{MN} *A shambles of Men's Flesh.*

Religions and Idols they have as many, as Nations and Humours; but the Devil hath the greatest part of their Devotions, whom all those Blacks do say, is white; for there are no Saints but Blacks.

{MN} But besides those great Kingdoms of *Congo, Angola,* and *Azichi,* in those unfrequented Parts are the Kingdoms of *Lango, Matania, Battua, Sofola, Mozambeche, Quivola,* the Isle of St. *Lawrence, Mombaza, Melinda,* the Empires of *Monomotapa, Monemugi,* and *Presbyter John,* with whom they have a kind of Trade, and their Rites, Customs, Climates, Temperatures, and Commodities by Relation. Also of great Lakes, that deserve the Names of Seas, and huge Mountains of divers sorts, as some scorched with heat, some covered with Snow; the Mountains of the Sun, also of the Moon, some of Chrystal, some of Iron, some of Silver, and Mountains of Gold, with the Original of *Nilus;* likewise sundry sorts of Cattel, Fishes, Fowls, strange Beasts, and monstrous Serpents; for Africa was always noted to be a fruitful Mother of such terrible Creatures; who meeting at their watering places, which are but Ponds in desart places, in regard of the heat of the Country, and their extremities of Nature, make strange Copulations, and so ingender those extraordinary Monsters. Of all these you may read in the History, of this *Edward Lopez,* translated into English by *Abraham Hartwel,* and dedicated to *John* Lord Archbishop of *Canterbury,* 1597. But because the Particulars are most concerning the conversion of those Pagans, by a good poor Priest, that first converted a Noble Man, to convert the King, and the rest of the Nobility; sent for so many Priests and Ornaments into *Portugal,* to Solemnize their Baptisms with such Magnificence, which was performed with such strange Curiosities, that those poor *Negro's* adored them as gods, till the Priests grew to that Wealth, a Bishop was sent to rule over them, which they would not endure, which endangered to spoil all before they could be reconciled. But not to trouble you too long with those Rarities of uncertainties; let us return again to *Barbary,* where the Wars being ended, and *Befferres* possessed of *Morocco,* and his Fathers Treasure, a new bruit arose amongst them, that *Muly Sidan* was raising an Army against him, who after took his Brother *Befferres* Prisoner; but by reason of the uncertainty, and the perfidious, treacherous, bloody murthers rather than War, amongst those perfidious, barbarous Moors, *Smith* returned with *Merham*, and the rest to *Saffe*, and so aboard his Ship, to try some other conclusions at Sea.

{MN} *Divers Nations yet unknown, and the wonders of* Africa.

CHAPTER. XX.

A brave Sea Fight betwixt to Spanish *Men of War, and Captain* Merham, *with* Smith.

MERHAM, a Captain of a Man of War then in the Road, invited Captain *Smith*, and two or three more of them aboard with him, where he spared not any thing he had to express his kindness, to bid them welcome, till it was too late to go on Shoar, so that necessity constrained them to stay aboard; a fairer Evening could not be, yet ere Midnight, such a Storm did arise, they were forced to let slip Cable, and Anchor, and put to Sea; spooning before the Wind, till they were driven to the *Canaries;* in the Calms they accommodated themselves, hoping this strange accident might yet produce some good event; not long it was before they took a small Bark coming from *Tenerif,* loaded with Wine; three or four more they chased, two they took, but found little in them, save a few Passengers, that told them of five *Dutch* Men of War, about the Isles, so that they stood for *Boiadora,* upon the *African* Shoar, betwixt which and *Cape Noa,* they descryed two Sail. *Merham* intending to know what they were, hailed them; very civilly they danced their Top-sails, and desired the Man of War to come aboard them, and take what he would, for they were but two poor distressed *Biskainers*. But *Merham* the old Fox, seeing himself in the Lions paws, sprung his louf, the other tacked after him, and came close up to his nether Quarter, gave his Broad-side, and so loufed up to Windward; the Vice-Admiral did the like, and at the next bout, the Admiral with a noise of Trumpets, and all his Ordnance, Murtherers, and Muskets, boarded him on his Broad-side, the other in like manner on his ley Quarter, that it was so dark, there was little light, but fire and smoak; long he stayed not, before he, fell off, leaving 4 or 5 of his Men sprawling over the Grating; after they had battered *Merham* about an hour, they boarded him again as before, and threw four Kedgars or Grapnels in Iron Chains, then shearing off, they thought so to have torn down the Grating; but the Admiral's Yard was so intangled in their Shrouds, *Merham* had time to discharge two cross barr shot amongst them, and divers Bolts of Iron made for that purpose, against his Bow, that made such a Breach, he feared they both mould have sunk for Company; so that the *Spaniard* was as yare in slipping his chained Grapnels, as *Merham* was in cutting the Tackling, kept fast their Yards in his Shrouds; the Vice-Admiral presently cleared himself, but spared neither his Ordnance nor Muskets to keep *Merham* from getting away, till the Admiral had repaired his Leak; from twelve at noon, till six at night, they thus interchanged one volly for another; then the Vice-Admiral fell on Stern, staying for the Admiral that came up again to him, and all that night stood after *Merham*, that shaped his course for *Mamora*, but such small way they made, the next Morning they were not three

Leagues off from *Cape Noa*. The two *Spanish* Men of War, for so they were, and well appointed, taking it in scorn as it seemed, with their Chase, Broadside, and Stern, the one after the other, within Musket shot, plying their Ordnance; and after an hours Work, commanded *Merham* amain for the King of Spain upon fair Quarter; *Merham* drank to them, and so discharged his Quarter Pieces. Which Pride the *Spaniard* to revenge, boarded him again, and many of them were got to the top to unsling the Main-Sail, which the Master and some others from the Round-House, caused to their cost to come tumbling down; about the Round-House the *Spaniards* so pestred, that they were forced to the great Cablen and blew it up; the smoak and fire was so vehement, as they thought the Ship on fire; they in the Fore-Castle were no less assaulted, that they blew up a piece of the Grating, with a great many of *Spaniards* more; then they cleared themselves with all speed, and *Merham* with as much Expedition to quench the Fire with wet Cloaths and Water, which began to grow too fast. The *Spaniard* still playing upon him with all the shot they could; the open Places presently they covered with old Sails, and prepared themselves to fight to the last Man. The Angry *Spaniard* seeing the fire quenched, hung out a Flag of truce to have but a Parley; but that desperate *Merham* knew there was but one way with him, and would have none, but the report of his Ordnance, which he did know well how to use for his best Advantage. Thus they spent the next Afternoon, and half the Night, when the *Spaniards* either lost them or left them. Seven and twenty Men *Merham* had slain and sixteen wounded, and could find they had received 140 great shot. A wounded *Spaniard* they kept alive confessed, they had lost 100 Men in the Admiral, which they did fear would sink ere she could recover a Port. Thus Re-accommodating their Sails, they failed for *Sancta Cruse, Cape Goa,* and *Magadore,* till they came again to *Safee,* and then he returned into England.

CHAPTER. XXI.

The continuation of the General History of Virginia; *the* Summer Isles, *and* New England; *with their present Estate from* 1624. *to this present* 1629.

CONCERNING these Countries, I would be sorry to trouble you with repeating one thing twice, as with their Mapps, Commodities, People, Government and Religion yet known; the beginning of these Plantations, their Numbers and Names, with the Names of the Adventures, the Yearly proceedings of every Governour both here and there. As for the Misprisions, Neglect, Grievances, and the causes of all these Rumours, losses and crosses that have happened; I refer you to the General History, where you shall find all this at large; especially to those Pages where you may read my Letter of Advice to the Councel and Company, what of necessity must be done, or lose all and leave the Country, Pag. 70. what Commodities I sent home, Pag. 163. my Opinion and offer to the Company, to feed and defend the Colonies, Pag. 150. my Account to them here of my Actions there, Pag. 163. and seven Answers to his Majesty's Commissioners: Seven Questions what hath hindered *Virginia,* and the remedy, Pag. 165. How those Noble Gentlemen spent near two Years in perusing all Letters came from thence; and the differences betwixt many Factions, both here and there, with their Complaints; especially about the *Sallery* which should have been a new Office in *London,* for the well ordering the sale of *Tobacco,* that 2500 Pounds should Yearly have been raised out of it, to pay four or five Hundred Pounds Yearly to the Governour of that Company, two or three Hundred to his Deputy; the rest into Stipends of forty or fifty Pounds Yearly for their Clerks and other Officers which were never there, Pag. 153. but not one Hundred Pounds for all them in *Virginia,* nor any thing for the most part of the Adventures in *England,* except the undertakers for the Lotteries, Setters out of Ships, Adventures of Commodities, also their Factors and many other Officers, there imployed only by friendship to raise their Fortunes out of the Labours of the true Industrious Planters by the Title of their Office, who under the colour of sincerity, did pillage and deceive all the rest most cunningly: For more than 150000 Pounds have been spent out of the Common Stock, besides many thousands have been there Consumed, and near 7000 People that there died, only for want of good Order and Government, otherwise long ere this there would have been more than 20000 People, where after twenty Years spent only in Complement and trying new Conclusions, was remaining scarce 1500, with some few Cattel.

Then the Company dissolved, but no Account of any thing; so that his Majesty appointed Commissioners to oversee, and give Order for their

Proceedings. Being thus in a manner left to themselves, since then within these four Years, you shall see how wonderfully they have increased beyond expectation; but so exactly as I desired, I cannot relate unto you: For altho' I have tired my self in seeking and discoursing with those returned thence, more than would a Voyage to *Virginia;* few can tell me any thing, but of that Place or Places they have Inhabited, and he is a great Traveller that hath gone up and down the River of *James* Town, been at *Pamaunk, Smith's* Isles, or *Accomack;* wherein for the most part, they keep one tune of their now particular abundance, and their former wants having been there, some sixteen Years, some twelve, some six, some near twenty, &c. But of their general Estate, or any thing of worth, the most of them doth know very little to any purpose.

{MN} Now the most I could understand in general, was from the Relation of Mr. *Nathaniel Cawsey,* that lived there with me, and returned *Anno Dom.* 1627. and some others affirm; Sir *George Yerely* was Governour, Captain *Francis West,* Doctor *John Pott,* Captain *Roger Smith,* Captain *Matthews,* Captain *Tucker,* Mr. *Clabourn,* and Mr. *Farrer,* of the Council: their Habitations many. The Governour, with two or three of the Council, are for most part at *James* Town, the rest repair thither as there is occasion; but every three Months they have a general Meeting, to consider of their Publick Affairs.

{MN} *Their estate* 1627.

{MN} Their Numbers then were about 1500, some say rather 2000, divided into seventeen or eighteen several Plantations; the greatest part thereof towards the falls, are so inclosed with Pallisadoes they regard not the *Salvages.* and amongst those Plantations above *James* Town, they have now found means to take plenty of Fish, as well with Lines as Nets, and where the Waters are the largest, having Means they need not want.

{MN} *Their numbers.*

{MN} Upon this River they seldom see any *Salvages,* but in the Woods, many times their Fires: yet some few there are, that upon their opportunity, have slain some few straglers, which have been revenged with the Death of so many of themselves; but no other Attempt hath been made upon them this two or three Years.

{MN} *Their condition with the Salvages.*

{MN} Their Cattel, Namely, Oxen, Kine, Bulls, they imagine to be about 2000; Goats great store and great increase; the wild Hoggs, which were infinite, are destroyed and eaten by the *Salvages:* but no Family is so poor that hath not tame Swine sufficient; and for Poultry, he is a very bad Husband, breedeth not an Hundred in a Year, and the Richer sort doth daily feed on them.

{MN} *Their increase of Cattel and Poultry.*

{MN} For Bread they have plenty, and so good, that those that make it well, better cannot be: Divers have much *English* Corn, especially Mr. *Abraham Perce,* which prepared this Year to sow two Hundred Acres of *English* Wheat, and as much with Barly, feeding daily about the number of sixty Persons at his own Charges.

{MN} *Plenty of Corn.*

{MN} For Drink, Some Malt the *Indian* Corn, others Barly, of which they make good Ale, both strong and small, and such plenty thereof, few of the Upper Planters drink any Water: but the better sort are well furnished with Sack, *Aquavitæ,* and good *English* Beer.

{MN} *Their Drink.*

{MN} The Servants commonly feed upon Milk Homili, which is bruised *Indian* Corn pounded, and boiled thick, and Milk for the sawce; but boiled with Milk, the best of all will feed oft on it, and leave their Flesh; with Milk, Butter and Cheese; with Fish, Bulls-flesh, for they seldom kill any other, &c. And every one is so applied to his labour about Tobacco and Corn, which doth yield them such Profit, they never regard any food from the *Salvages,* nor have they any Trade or Conference with them, but upon meer Accidents and Defiances: And now the Merchants have left it, there having gone so many voluntary Ships within these two Years, as have furnished them with Apparel, Sack, *Aquavitæ,* and all necessaries, much better than any before.

{MN} *Their Servants diet.*

{MN} For Arms, There is scarce any Man but he is furnished with a Piece, a Jack, a Coat of Male, a Sword or Rapier; and every Holy-day, every Plantation doth Exercise their Men in Arms, by which means Hunting and Fowling, the most part of them are most Excellent Marks-men.

{MN} *Their Arms and Exercise.*

{MN} For Discoveries they have made none, nor any other Commodity than Tobacco do they apply themselves unto, tho' never any was Planted at first. And whereas the Countrey was heretofore held most intemperate and contagious by many, now they have Houses, Lodgings, Victuals, and the Sun hath Power to Exhale up the moist Vapours of the Earth, where they have cut down the Wood, which before it could not, being covered with spreading tops of high Trees; they find it much more healthful than before; nor for their Numbers, few Countries are less troubled with Death, Sickness, or any other Disease, nor where overgrown Women become more fruitful.

{MN} *Their Health and Discoveries.*

{MN-1} Since this, Sir *George Yerely* died 1628, Captain *West* Succeeded him; but about a Year after, returned for *England.* Now Doctor *Poor* is Governour, and the rest of the Council as before: *James* Town is yet their chief Seat, most of the Wood destroyed, little Corn there Planted, but all Converted into Pasture and Gardens, wherein doth grow all manner of Herbs and Roots we have in *England,* in abundance, and as good Grass as can be. Here most of their Cattle do feed, their Owners being most some one way, some another, about their Plantations, and return again when they please, or any Shipping comes in to Trade. Here in the Winter they have Hay for their Cattel, but in other Places they Browze upon Wood, and the great husks of their Corn, with some Corn in them, doth keep them well. {MN-2} Mr. *Hutchins* saith, they have 2000 Cattle, and about 5000 People, but *Master Floud, John Davis, William Emerson,* and divers others say, about 5000 People, and 5000 Kine, Calves, Oxen and Bulls; for Goats, Hoggs and Poultry, Corn, Fish, Dear, and many sorts of other wild Beasts; and Fowl in their Season, they have so much more than they spend, they are able to feed three or four Hundred more than they have; and do oft much relieve many Ships, both there, and for their Return; and this last Year was there at least two or three and Twenty Sale. They have oft much Salt-fish from *New England,* but fresh Fish enough, when they will take it; Peaches in abundance at *Kecoughtan;* Apples, Pears, Apricocks, Vines, Figgs, and other Fruits some have Planted that prospered exceedingly, but their Diligence about Tobacco, left them to be spoiled by the Cattel, yet now they begin to Revive; {MN-3} Mrs. *Pearce,* an Honest Industrious Woman, hath been there near twenty Years, and now returned, saith, she hath a Garden at *James* Town, containing three or four Acres, where in one Year she hath gathered near an Hundred Bushels of excellent Figgs; and that of her own Provision she can keep a better House in *Virginia,* than here in *London* for 3 or 400 Pounds a Year, yet went thither with little or nothing.

They have some tame Geese, Ducks and Turkies. The Masters now do so train up their Servants and Youth in shooting Deer and Fowl, that the Youths will kill them as well as their Masters. They have two Brew-houses, but they find the *Indian* Corn so much better than ours, they begin to leave sowing it. Their Cities and Towns are only scattered Houses, they call Plantations, as are our Country Villages; but no Ordnance Mounted. The Forts Captain *Smith* left a Building, so ruined, there is scarce Mention where they were; no Discoveries of any thing more, than the curing of Tobacco, by which hitherto, being so present a Commodity of Gain, it hath brought them to this abundance; but that they are so disjointed, and every one Commander of himself to Plant what he will: {MN-4} they are now so well provided, that they are able to subsist; and if they would join together, now to work upon Soap, Ashes, Iron, Rape-Oil, Mader, Pitch and Tarr, Flax and Hemp; as for their Tobacco, there comes from many Places such abundance, and the charge so great, it is not worth the bringing home.

{MN-1} *The present estate of* Virginia 1629.

{MN-2} *Mr.* Hutchins. *Five thousand people. Five thousand Cattel. Goats, Hogs, and Poultry infinite.*

{MN-3} *Good Hospitality.*

{MN-4} *Commodities worth making, Black Wallnut, Also for Pikes, Oak for Planks, knees for ships, Cypress, for Chests, &c.*

There is gone, and now a going, divers Ships, as Captain *Perse,* Captain *Prine,* with Sir *John Harvey* to be their Governour, with two or three Hundred People; there is also some from *Bristow,* and other Parts of the West Country a preparing, which I heartily pray to God to Bless, and send them a Happy and Prosperous Voyage.

Nathaniel Causie, Master *Hutchins,* Master *Floud, John Davis, William Emerson,* Master *William Barnet,* Master *Cooper,* and others.

CHAPTER. XXII.

The proceedings and present estate of the Summer Isles, *from* Anno Dom. 1624, *to this present* 1629.

FROM the *Summer Isles,* Mr. *Ireland,* and divers others report, their Forts, Ordnance and Proceedings, are much as they were in the Year 1622. as you may read in the General History, Pag. 199. Captain *Woodhouse* Governour. There are few sorts of any Fruits in the West Indies, but they grow there in abundance; yet the fertility of the Soil in many Places decayeth, being Planted every Year, for their Plantains, which is a most delicate Fruit, they have lately found a way by Pickling or Drying them, to bring them over into *England,* there being no such Fruit in *Europe,* and wonderful for increase. For Fish, Flesh, Figgs, Wine, and all sorts of most excellent Herbs, Fruits and Roots they have in abundance. In this Governour's time, a kind of Whale, or rather a Jubarta, was driven on Shoar in *Southampton* Tribe from the West, over an Infinite Number of Rocks so bruised, that the Water in the Bay where she lay, was all Oily, and the Rocks about it all Bedasht with Parmacitty, congealed like Ice, a good quantity we gathered, with which we commonly cured any Boil, Hurt or Bruise; some burnt it in their Lamps, which blowing out, the very snuff will burn so long as there is any of the Oil remaining, for two or three days together. {MN}

{MN} *The present Estate of the* Summer Isles.

The next Governour was Captain *Philip Bell,* whose time being expired, Captain *Roger Wood* possess'd his Place, a worthy Gentleman of good desert, and hath lived a long time in the Country; their Numbers are about 2 or 3000 Men, Women and Children, who increase there exceedingly; their greatest Complaint is want of Apparel, and too much Custom, and too many Officers; the Pity is, there are no more Men than Women, yet no great Mischief, because there is so much less Pride: the Cattle they have increase exceedingly; their Forts are well maintain'd by the Merchants here, and Planters there; to be brief, this Isle is an excellent Bit to Rule a great Horse.

All the Cohow Birds and Egbirds are gone; seldom any wild Catts seen; no Rats to speak off; but the Worms are yet very troublesome; the People very healthful, and the Ravens gone; Fish enough, but not so near the shoar as it used, by the much beating it; it is an Isle that hath such a Rampire and a Ditch, and for the quantity so manned, Victualled, and Fortified, as few in the World do exceed it, or is like it.

{MN} The 22d of March, two Ships came from thence; the *Peter-Bonaventure,* near 200 Tunns, and sixteen Pieces of Ordnance; the Captain, *Thomas Sherwin;* the Master, Mr. *Edward Some,* like him in Condition, a Goodly, Lusty, Proper, Valiant Man: The *Lydia,* wherein was Mr. *Anthony Thorne,* a smaller Ship, were chased by eleven Ships of *Dunkirk;* being thus over-match'd, Captain *Sherwin* was taken by them in *Torbay,* only his Valiant Master was slain; the Ship with about seventy *English* Men they carried betwixt *Dover* and *Callais* to *Dunkirk;* but the *Lydia* safely recovered *Dartmouth.*

{MN} *An Evil Mischance.*

These Noble Adventures for all thole losses patiently do bear them; but they hope the King and State will understand it is worth keeping, tho' it afford nothing but Tobacco, and that now worth little or nothing, Custom and Fraught pay'd, yet it is worth keeping, and not supplanting; tho' great Men feel not those losses, yet Gardiners, Carpenters and Smiths, do pay for it.

From the Relation of *Robert Chestevan* and others.

CHAPTER. XXIII.

The Proceedings and present Estate of New England, *since* 1624. *to this present* 1629.

WHEN I went first to the North part of *Virginia,* where the Westerly Colony had been planted, it had dissolved it self within a Year, and there was not one *Christian* in all the Land. I was set forth at the sole Charge of four Merchants of *London;* the Country being then reputed by your Westerlings, a most Rocky Barren, Desolate Desart; {MN-1} but the good Return brought from thence, with the Maps and Relations I made of the Country, which I made so manifest, some of them did believe me, and they were well embraced both by the *Londoners* and the *Westerlings,* for whom I had promised to undertake it, I thinking to have joined them all together, but that might well have been a work of *Hercules.* Betwixt them long there was much contention; the *Londoners* indeed went bravely forward; but in three or four Years, I and my Friends consumed many hundred Pounds amongst the *Plimothians,* who only fed me with delays, promises and excuses, but no Performance of any thing to any purpose. In the interim, many particular Ships went thither, and finding my Relations true, and that I had not taken that I brought home from the *French* Men, as had been reported; yet further, for my Pains to discredit me, and my calling it *New-England,* they obscured, and shadowed it, with the Title of *Canada,* till at my humble suit, it pleased our most Royal King *Charles,* whom God long keep, bless and preserve, then Prince of *Wales,* to confirm it with my Map and Book, by the Title of *New England;* the gain thence returning, did make the same thereof so increase, that thirty, forty, or fifty sail went Yearly only to Trade and Fish; but nothing would be done for a Plantation, till about some Hundred of your Brownists of *England, Amsterdam* and *Leyden,* went to *New Plimouth,* whose humorous Ignorances, caused them for more than a Year to endure a wonderful deal of misery, with an infinite patience; saying my Books and Maps were much better cheap to teach them than my self; {MN-2} many other have used the like good Husbandry, that have payed soundly in trying their self-will'd conclusions; but those in time doing well, divers others have in small handfuls undertaken to go there, to be several Lords and Kings of themselves, but most vanished to nothing; notwithstanding the Fishing Ships, made such good returns, at last it was ingrossed by twenty Patentees, that divided my Map into twenty parts, and cast Lots for their shares; but Money not coming in as they expected, procured a Proclamation, none should go thither without their Licences to Fish; but for every thirty Tuns of Shipping, to pay them five Pounds; besides, upon great Penalties, neither to Trade with the Natives, cut down Wood for their Stages, without giving satisfaction, though all the Country is nothing but Wood, and none to make use of it, with many such other pretences, for to make this Country plant it self, by its own Wealth: Hereupon most Men grew so discontented, that few or none would go; so that the Patentees, who never a one of them had been there, seeing those Projects Would not prevail, have since not hindred any to go that would, that within these few last years, more have gone thither than ever.

{MN-1} *Considerations about the loss of time.*

{MN-2} *The effect of negardliness.*

{MN} Now this Year 1629, a great company of People of good Rank, Zeal, Means, and Quality, have made a great Stock, and with six good Ships in the Months of April and May, they set Sail from *Thames*, for the Bay of the *Massachusets*, otherwise called *Charles's* River; *viz.* the *George Bonaventure*, of twenty pieces of Ordnance, the *Talbot* nineteen, the *Lions-whelp* eight, the *May-flower* fourteen, the *Four Sisters* fourteen, the *Pilgrim* four, with three hundred and fifty Men, Women, and Children; also an hundred and fifteen head of Cattel, as Horse, Mares, and neat Beast; one and forty Goats, some Conies, with all Provision for Houshold and Apparel; six pieces of great Ordnance for a Fort, with Muskets, Pikes, Corselets, Drums, Colours, with all Provision necessary for a Plantation, for the good of Man; other Particulars I understand of no more, than is writ in the general History of those Countries.

{MN} *A new Plantation* 1629.

But you are to understand, that the noble Lord chief Justice *Popham*, Judge *Doderege;* the Right Honourable Earls of *Pembroke, Southampton, Salisbury,* and the rest, as I take it, they did all think, as I and them went with me, did; That had those two Countries been planted, as it was intended, that no other Nation should complant betwixt us. If ever the King of *Spain* and we should fall foul, those Countries being so capable of all Materials for shipping, by this might have been Owners of a good Fleet of Ships, and to have relieved a whole Navy from *England* upon occasion; yea, and to have furnished *England* with the most Easterly Commodities; and now since, seeing how conveniently the *Summer Isles* fell to our shares, so near the *West-Indies*, we might with much more facility than the *Dutch* Men have invaded the *West-Indies*, that doth now put in practice, what so long hath been advised on, by many an honest *English* States-man.

{MN} Those Countries, Captain *Smith* oft times used to call his Children that never had Mother; and well he might, for few Fathers ever payed dearer for so little content; and for those that would truly understand, how many strange Accidents hath befallen them and him; how oft up, how oft down, sometimes near despair, and ere long flourishing, cannot but conceive Gods infinite Mercies and Favours towards them. Had his Designs been to have perswaded Men to a Mine of Gold, though few doth conceive either the charge or pains in refining it, nor the power nor care to defend it; or some new Invention to pass to the South Sea, or some strange Plot to invade some strange Monastery, or some portable Country, or some chargeable Fleet to take some rich Carocks in the *East-Indies;* of Letters of Mart to rob some poor Merchants; What multitudes of both People and Money would contend to be first imployed? But in those noble endeavours (now) how few of quality, unless it be to beg some Monopoly; and those seldom seek the common good, but the Commons Goods, as you may read at large in his general History, *pag.* 217, 218, 219, his general Observations and Reasons for this Plantation; for yet those Countries are not so forward, but they may become as miserable as ever, if better courses be not taken than is; as this *Smith* will plainly demonstrate to his Majesty, or any other noble Person of Ability, liable generously to undertake it; how within a Short time to make *Virginia* able to resist any Enemy, that as yet lieth open to all, and yield the King more Custom within these few years, in certain staple Commodities, than ever it did in Tobacco; which now not being worth bringing home, the Custom will be as uncertain to the King, as dangerous to the Plantation.

{MN} *Notes of inconveniency.*

CHAPTER. XXIV.

A brief Discourse of divers Voyages made unto the goodly Country of Guinea *and the great River of the* Amazons; *relating also the present Plantation there.*

IT IS NOT unknown how that most Industrious and honourable Knight, Sir *Walter Rawleigh*, in the Year of Our Lord 1595, taking the Isle of *Trinidado*, fell with the Coast of *Guiana*, Northward of the Line 10 degrees, and coasted the Coast, and searched up the River *Oranoco;* where understanding that twenty several Voyages had been made by the Spaniards; in discovering this Coast and River, to find a passage to the great City of *Mano*, called by them the *Eldorado*, or the Golden City: he did his utmost to have found some better Satisfaction than Relations: {MN-1} But means failing him, he left his trusty Servant *Francis Sparrow* to seek it, who wandring up and down those Countries, some fourteen or fifteen years, unexpectedly returned; I have heard him say, he was led blinded into this City by *Indians;* but little Discourse of any purpose, touching the largeness of the report of it; his body seeming as a Man of an uncurable Consumption, shortly died here after in *England*. There are above thirty fair Rivers that fall into the Sea, between the River of *Amazons* and *Oranoco*, which are some nine degrees asunder. {MN-2} In the year 1605, Captain *Ley*, Brother to that noble Knight, Sir *Oliver Ley*, with divers others, planted himself in the River *Weapoco*, wherein I should have been a Party; but he died, and there lies buried, and the supply miscarrying, the rest escaped as they could.

{MN-1} Sparrow *left to seek the great city of* Mano.

{MN-2} Captain *Charles Ley*.

{MN} Sir *Thomas Roe*, known to be a most Noble Gentleman, before he went Lord Ambassadour to the Great *Mogul*, or the Great *Turk*, spent a year or two upon this Coast, and about the River of the *Amazons*, {MN-2} wherein he most imployed Captain *Matthew Morton*, an expert Sea-man in the discovery of this famous River, a Gentleman that was the first shot, and mortally supposed wounded to Death, with me in *Virginia*, yet since hath been twice with command in *East-Indies;* {MN-3} Also Captain *William White*, and divers others worthy and industrious Gentlemen, both before and since, hath spent much time and charge to discover it more perfectly, but nothing more effected for a Plantation, till it was undertaken by Captain *Robert Harcote* 1609.

{MN-1} Sir *Thomas Roe*.

{MN-2} Captain *Morton*.

{MN-3} Captain *White*.

{MN} This worthy Gentleman, after he had by Commission made a discovery to his mind, left his Brother *Michael Harcote*, with some fifty or sixty Men in the River *Weapoco*, and so presently returned to *England*, where he obtained by the favour of Prince *Henry* a large Patent for all that Coast called *Guiana*, together with the famous River of *Amazons*, to him and his Heirs: but so many troubles here surprized him, though he did his best to supply them, he was not able, only some few he sent over as Passengers, with certain *Dutch* Men, but to small purpose. Thus this business lay dead for divers years, till Sir *Walter Rawleigh*, accompanied with many valiant Soldiers and brave Gentlemen, went his last Voyage to *Guiana*, amongst the which, was Captain *Roger North*, Brother to the Right Honourable the Lord *Dudley North*, who upon this Voyage, having stayed, and seen divers Rivers upon this Coast, took such a liking to those Countries, having had before this Voyage, more perfect and particular Information of the excellency of the great River of the *Amazons*, above any of the rest, by certain *English* Men returned so rich, from thence in good Commodities, they would not go with Sir *Walter Rawleigh* in search of Gold; that after his return for *England*, he endeavoured by his best Abilities to interest his Country and State in those fair Regions, which by the way of Letters Patents unto divers Noble Men and Gentlemen of Quality, erected into a Company and Perpetuity for Trade and Plantation, not knowing of the Interest of Captain *Harcote*.

{MN} Captain *Harcote*.

{MN} Whereupon accompanied with 120 Gentlemen and others, with a Ship, a Pinnace and two Shallops, to remain in the Country, he set Sail from *Plimouth* the last of *April* 1620, and within seven Weeks after he arrived well in the *Amazons*, only with the loss of one old Man: Some hundred Leagues they ran up the River to settle his Men, where the sight of the Country and People so contented them, that never Men thought themselves more happy: Some *English* and *Irish* that had lived there some eight years, only supplied by the *Dutch*, he reduced to his Company and to leave the *Dutch*: having made a good Voyage, to the value of more than the charge, he returned to *England* with divers good Commodities, besides, Tobacco: So that it may well be conceived, that if this Action had not been thus crossed the Generality of *England* had by this time been won and encouraged therein. But the time was not yet come, that God would have this great business effected, by reason of the great Power the Lord *Gundamore*, Ambassadour for the King of *Spain*, had in *England,* to cross and ruin those Proceedings, and so unfortunate Captain *North* was on this business, he was twice committed Prisoner to the Tower, and the Goods detained, till they were spoiled, who beyond all others, was by much the greatest Adventurer and Loser.

{MN} Captain *Roger North.*

{MN} Notwithstanding all this, those that he had left in the *Amazons,* would not abandon the Country. Captain *Thomas Painton,* a worthy Gentleman; his Lieutenant dead. Captain *Charles Parker,* Brother to the Right Honourable the Lord *Morley,* lived there six years after; Mr. *John Christmas,* five years; so well, they would not return, although they might, with divers other Gentlemen of Quality and others: All thus destitute of any supplies from *England.* But all Authority being dissolved, want of Government did more wrong their Proceedings, than all other crosses whatsoever. Some relief they had sometime from the *Dutch,* who knowing their Estates, gave what they pleased, and took what they list. Two Brothers, Gentlemen, *Thomas* and *William Hixon,* who stayed three years there, are now gone to stay in the *Amazons,* in the Ships lately sent thither.

{MN} *Nota bene.*

The business thus remaining in this fort, three private Men left of that Company, named Mr. *Thomas Warriner, John Rhodes,* and *Robert Bims,* having lived there about two years, came for *England,* and to be free from the disorders that did grow in the *Amazons,* for want of Government amongst their Country-men, and to be quiet amongst themselves, made means to let themselves out for St. *Christophers;* their whole number being but fifteen Persons that payed for their Passage in a Ship going for *Virginia,* where they remained a year before they were supplied, and then that was but four or five Men. Thus this Isle, by this small beginning, having no interruption by their own Country, hath not got the start of the Continent and main Land of *Guinea,* which hath been laid apart, and let alone until that Captain *North,* ever watching his best opportunity and advantage of time in the State, hath now again pursued, and set on foot his former design. Captain *Harcote* being now willing to surrender his Grant, and to joyn with Captain *North,* in passing a new Patent, and to erect a Company for Trade and Plantation in the *Amazons,* and all the Coast and Country of *Guinea* for ever. Whereupon, they have sent this present year in *January,* and since 1628, four Ships, with near two hundred Persons; the first Ship with 112 Men, not one miscarried; the rest went since, not yet heard of and are preparing another with their best Expedition; and since *January* is gone from *Holland,* 100 *English* and *Irish,* conducted by the old Planters.

This great River lieth under the Line, the two chief Head Lands North and South, are about three degrees asunder, the mouth of it is so full of many great and small Isles, it is an easie matter for an unexperienced Pilot to lose his way. It is held one of the greatest Rivers in *America,* and as most Men think in the World; and cometh down with such a fresh, it maketh the Sea fresh, more than thirty Miles from the Shoar. Captain *North* having seated his Men about an hundred Leagues in the Main, sent Captain *William White,* with thirty Gentlemen and others, in a Pinnace of thirty Tun, to discover further, which they did some two hundred Leagues, where they found the River to divide it self in two parts, till then all full of Islands, and a Country most healthful, pleasant and fruitful; for they found food enough, and all returned safe and in good health: In this discovery, they saw many Towns well inhabited, some with three hundred People, some with five, six, or seven hundred; and of some they understood to be of so many thousands, most differing very much, especially in their Languages: Whereof they suppose by those *Indians,* they understand are many hundreds more, unfrequented till then by any *Christian,* most of them stark naked, both Men, Women and Children, but they saw not any such Giant-like Women as the Rivers name importeth. But for those where Captain *North* hath seated his Company, it is not known where Indians were ever so kind to any Nation, not sparing any pains, danger or labour, to feed and maintain them. The *English* following their Buildings, Fortifications and Sugar-works; for which they have sent most expert Men, and with them all things necessary for that purpose; to effect which, they want not the help of those kind Indians to produce; and many other good Commodities, which (God willing) will ere long make plain and apparent to this Kingdom, and all the Adventures and Well-willers to this Plantation, to be well worthy the cherishing and following with all alacrity.

CHAPTER. XXV.

The Beginning and Proceedings of the new Plantation of St. Christopher *by Captain* Warner.

MASTER *Ralph Merifield* and others, having furnished this worthy Industrious Gentleman, {MN-1} he arrived at St. *Christophers,* as is said, with fifteen Men, the 28th of *January* 1623, *viz. William Tested, John Rhodes, Robert Bints,* Mr. *Benifield,* Sergeant *Jones,* Mr. *Ware, William Ryle, Rowland Grascock,* Mr. *Bond,* Mr. *Langley,* Mr. *Weaver, Edward Warner,* their Captain's Son, and now Deputy Governour, till his Father's return, Sergeant *Aplon,* one Sailor and a Cook: At their arrival, they found three *French* Men, who sought to oppose Captain *Warner,* and to set the *Indians* upon us; but at last we all became Friends, and lived with the *Indians* a Month, then we built a Fort, and a House, and planting Fruits, by *September* we made a crop of Tobacco; {MN-2} but upon the nineteenth of *September* came a *Hericano* and blew it away, all this while we lived upon Cassada Bread, Potatoes, Plantanes, Pines, Turtles, Guanes, and Fish plenty; for drink we had *Nicnobby.*

{MN-1} 1623.

{MN-2} *A Hericano.*

{MN} The 18th March 1624 arrived Captain *Jefferson,* with three Men Passengers in the *Hopewell* of *London,* with some Trade for the *Indians,* and then we had another crop of Tobacco, in the mean time the *French* had planted themselves in the other end of the Isle; with this crop Captain *Warner* returned for *England* in *September* 1625.

{MN} 1624.

In his absence came in a *French* Pinnace, under the command of *Monsieur de Nombe,* that told us, the *Indians* had slain some *French* Men in other of the *Caribbe* Isles, and that there were six Peryagoes, which are huge great Trees, formed as your Canoos, but so laid out on the sides with Boards, they will seem like a little Gally: {MN} Six of those, with about four or five hundred strange *Indians* came unto us, we bade them be gone, but they would not; whereupon we and the *French* joyned together, and upon the fifth of *November* set upon them, and put them to flight: upon New years Even they came again, found three *English* going about the Isle, whom they slew.

{MN} *Their Fight with the* Indians.

{MN-1} Until the fourth of *August*, we stood upon our Guard, living upon the spoil and did nothing. But now Captain *Warner* arriving again with near an hundred People, then we fell to work and planting as before; {MN-2} but upon the fourth of September, came such a Hericano, as blew down all our Houses, Tobacco, and two Drums into the air we know not whither, drove two Ships on Shoar that were both split; all our Provision thus lost, we were very miserable, living only on what we could get in the wild Woods, {MN-3} we made a small party of French and English to go aboard for Provision, but in their returning home, eight *French* Men were slain in the Harbour.

{MN-1} 1625.

{MN-2} *A Hericano.*

{MN-3} *Eight French Slain.*

{MN} Thus we continued till near *June* that the *Tortles* came in 1627, but the French being like to starve, sought to surprize us, and all the Cassado, Potatoes, and Tobacco we had planted, but we did prevent them. The 26th of *October*, came in Captain *William Smith*, in the *Hope-well*, with some Ordnance, Shot and Powder, from the Earl of *Carlisle*, with Captain *Pelham* and thirty Men; about that time also came the *Plow*, also a small Ship of *Bristow*, with Captain *Warner's* Wife, and six or seven Women more.

{MN} 1627.

{MN} Upon the 25th of *November*, the *Indians* set upon the French, for some injury about their Women, and slew six and twenty *French* Men, five *English*, and three *Indians*. Their Weapons are Bows and Arrows, their Bows are never bent, but the string lies flat to the Bow; their Arrows a small Reed, four or five foot long, headed some with the poisoned Sting of the Tail of a Stingray, some with Iron, some with Wood, but all so poisoned, that if they draw but blood, the hurt is incurable.

{MN} *Three* Indians *Slain.*

{MN} The next day came in Captain *Charles Saltonstall*, a young Gentleman, Son of Sir *Samuel Saltonstall*, who brought with him good store of all Commodities to relieve the Plantation; but by reason some *Hollanders*, and others had been there lately before him, who carried away with them all the

Tobacco, he was forced to put away all his Commodities upon trust till the next crop; in the mean time he resolved there to stay, and imploy himself and his Company in planting Tobacco, hoping thereby to make a Voyage, but before he could be ready to return for *England,* a *Hericano* happening, his Ship was split, to his great loss, being sole Merchant and owner himself, notwithstanding forced to pay to the Governour the fifth part of his Tobacco, and for fraught to *England,* three pence a pound, and nine pence a pound custom, which amounts together to more than threescore pound in the hundred pound, to the great discouragement of him and many others, that intended well to those Plantations. Nevertheless he is gone again this present year 1629, with a Ship of about three hundred Tuns, and very near two hundred People, with Sir *William Tuffton* Governour for the *Barbadoes,* and divers Gentlemen, and all manner of Commodities fit for a Plantation.

{MN} *The arrival of many English Ships.*

Captain *Prinn,* Captain *Stone,* and divers others came in about *Christmas;* so that this last year, there hath been about thirty Sail of *English, French,* and *Dutch* Ships, and all the *Indians* forced out of the Isle, for they had done much mischief amongst the *French,* in cutting their Throats, burning their Houses, and spoiling their Tobacco; amongst the rest *Tegramund,* a little Child, the King's Son, his Parents being slain, or fled, was by great chance saved, and carefully brought to *England,* by Master *Merifield,* who brought him from thence, and bringeth him up as his own Children.

{MN-1} It lieth seventeen degrees Northward of the Line, about an hundred and twenty Leagues from the *Cape de tres Puntas,* the nearest main Land in *America,* it is about eight Leagues in length, and four in breadth; an Island amongst 100 Isles in the *West Indies,* called the *Caribbes,* where ordinarily all them that frequent the *West Indies,* refresh themselves; those, most of them are Rocky, little, and Mountainous, yet frequented with the *Canibals;* many of them inhabited, as Saint *Domingo,* Saint *Mattalin,* Saint *Lucia,* Saint *Vincent, Granada,* and *Margarita,* to the Southward; Northward, none but Saint *Christophers,* and it but lately, yet they will be ranging *Marigalanta, Guardalupo, Deceado, Mountserat, Antegua, Mevis, Bernardo,* Saint *Martin,* and Saint *Bartholomew,* but the worst of the four Isles possessed by the *Spaniard,* as *Portorico* or *Jamaica,* is better than them all; as for *Hispaniola,* and *Cuba,* they are worthy the Title of two rich Kingdoms, the rest not respected by the *Spaniards,* for want of Harbours, and their better choice of good Land, and profit in the main. But Captain *Warner,* having been very familiar with Captain *Painton,* in the *Amazon,* hearing his information of this St. *Christophers;* and having made a years trial, as it is said, returned for *England,* joyning with Master *Merifield* and his Friends, got Letters Patents from King James to plant and possess it. Since then, the Right Honourable the Earl of *Carlisle* hath got Letters Patents also, not only of that, but all the *Caribe* Isles about it, who is now chief Lord of them, and the *English* his Tenants that do possess them; over whom he appointeth such Governours and Officers as their affairs require; and although there be a great Custom imposed upon them, considering their other charges, both to feed and maintain themselves; yet there is there, and now a going, near upon the number of three thousand People; where by reason of the rockiness and thickness of the Woods in the Isle, it is difficult to pass, and such a snuff of the Sea goeth on the Shoar, ten may better defend, than fifty assault. {MN-2} In this Isle are many Springs, but yet Water is scarce again in many places; the Valleys and sides of the Hills very fertile, but the Mountains harsh, and of a sulphurous composition; all overgrown with *Palmetas, Cotten* Trees; *Lignum vitæ*, and divers other sorts, but none like any in Christendom, except those carried thither; the air very pleasant and healthful, but exceeding hot, yet so tempered with cool breaths, it seems very temperate to them, that are little used to it; the Trees being always green, the days and nights always very near equal in length, always Summer; only they have in their Seasons great Gusts and Rains, and sometimes a Hericano, which is an over grown, and a most violent storm.

{MN-1} *The Description of the Isle.*

{MN-2} *The Springs; Temper; and Seasons.*

{MN} In some of those Isles, are Cattel, Goats, and Hogs, but here none but what they must carry; *Guanes* they have, which is a little harmless Beast, like a *Crocodile*, or *Alligator*, very fat and good Meat; she lays Eggs in the Sand, as doth the Land Crabs, which live here In abundance, like Conies in Boroughs, unless about *May*, when they come down to the Sea side, to lay in the Sand, as the other; and all their Eggs are hatched by the heat of the Sun.

{MN} *A strange hatching of eggs for beasts.*

{MN} From *May* to *September*, they have good store of Tortoises that come out of the Sea to lay their Eggs in the Sand, and are hatched as the other; they will lay half a peck at a time, and near a bushel ere they have done, and are round like Tenis-balls: This Fish is like Veal in taste, the Fat of a brownish colour, very good and wholsom. We seek them in the Nights, where we find them on shoar, we turn them upon their backs, till the next day we fetch them home, for they can never return themselves, being so hard, a Cart may go over them, and so big, one will suffice forty or fifty Men to dinner. Divers sorts of other Fish they have in abundance, and *Prawenes* most great and excellent, but none will keep sweet scarce twelve hours.

{MN} *Fish.*

{MN} The best and greatest is a *Passer Flaminga,* which walking at her length, is as tall as a Man; *Pigeons* and *Turtle Doves* in abundance; some *Parrots,* wild *Hawks,* but divers other sorts of good Sea-fowl, whose Names we know not.

{MN} *Birds.*

{MN} *Cassado* is a Root planted in the Ground, of a wonderful Increase, and will make very good White-bread, but the Juce Rank Poyson, yet boyled, better than Wine; *Potatoes, Cabbages,* and *Radish* plenty.

{MN} *Roots.*

{MN} Maize, like the *Virginia* Wheat; we have Pine-Apple, near so big as an Hartichock, but the most daintiest taste of any Fruit; *Plantains,* an excellent and most increasing Fruit; Apples, Prickle Pears, and Pease, but differing all from ours. There is Pepper that groweth in a little red Husk, as big as a Walnut, about four Inches in length, but the long Cods are small, and much stronger and better for use, than that from the *East Indies.* There is too sorts of Cotten, the silk Cotten as in the *East Indies,* groweth upon a small stalk, as good for Beds as Down; the other upon a shrub, and beareth a Cod bigger than a Walnut, full of Cotten wool: Anotto also groweth upon a shrub, with a Cod like the other, and nine or ten on a bunch, full of Anotto, very good for Dyers, tho' wild; Sugar Canes, not tame, four or five foot high; also Mastick, and Locus-trees; great and hard Timber, Gourds, Musk-Melons, Water-Melons, Lettice, Parsly; all places naturally bear Purslain of it self; Sope-berries like a Musquet Bullet, that washeth as white as Sope; in the middle of the Root is a thing like a Sedge, a very good Fruit, we call Pengromes; a Pappaw is as great as an Apple, coloured like an Orange, and good to eat, a small hard Nut, like a Hazel Nut, grows close to the Ground, and like this grows on the Palmetas, which we call a Mucca Nut; Mustard-seed will grow to a great Tree, but bears no seed, yet the Leaves will make good Mustard; the Mancinel Tree, the Fruit is Poison; good Figs in abundance; but the Palmeta serveth to build Forts and Houses, the Leaves to cover them, and many other uses; the juice we draw from them, till we suck them to Death, (is held restorative) and the top for meat doth serve us as Cabbage; but oft we want Powder'd Beef and Bacon, and many other needful necessaries.

{MN} *Fruits.*

By *Thomas Simons, Rowland Grascocke, Nicholas Burgh,* and others.

CHAPTER. XXVI.

The first Planting of the Barbadoes.

THE *BARBADOS* lies South-West and by South, an hundred Leagues from St. *Christophers,* threescore Leagues West and South from *Trinidado,* and some fourscore Leagues from *Cape de Salinos,* the next part of the main. The first Planters brought thither by Captain *Henry Powel,* were forty *English,* with seven or eight *Negros;* then he went to *Disacuba* in the main, where he got thirty *Indians,* Men, Women and Children of the *Arawacos,* Enemies both to the *Caribbes* and the *Spaniards.* {MN} The Isle is most like a Triangle, each side forty or fifty Miles square, some exceeding great Rocks, but the most part exceeding good Ground; abounding with an infinite number of Swine, some Turtles, and many sorts of excellent Fish; many great Ponds wherein is Duck and Mallard; excellent Clay for Pots, Wood and Stone for Building, and a Spring near the midst of the Isle of *Bitume,* which is a liquid mixture like Tarr, that by the great Rains falls from the Tops of the Mountains, it floats upon the Water in such abundance, that drying up, it remains like great Rocks of Pitch, and as good as Pitch for any use.

{MN} *A Description of the Isle.*

{MN} The Mancinel Apple, is of a most pleasant sweet smell, of the bigness of a Crab, but rank Poyson, yet the Swine and Birds have wit to shun it; great store of exceeding great Locus-trees, two or three Fathom about, of a great height, that beareth a Cod full of Meal, will make Bread in time of necessity. A Tree like a Pine beareth a Fruit so great as a Musk Melon, which hath always ripe Fruit Flowers, or Green Fruit, which will refresh two or three Men, and very comfortable; Plumb-trees many, the Fruit great and Yellow, which but strained into Water in four and twenty hours, will be very good drink; wild Figg-trees there are many; all those Fruits do fat the Hoggs, yet at sometimes of the Year they are so lean as Carrion; Guane-trees bear a Fruit so big as a Pear, good and wholsom; Palmetaes of three several sorts; Pappaws, Prickle Pears, good to eat or make drink; Cedar Trees very tall and great; Fustick Trees are very great, and the wood yellow, good for dying; Soap Berries, the kernel so big as a sloe, and good to eat; Pumpeons in abundance; Goads so great as will make good great Bottles, and cut in two pieces, good Dishes and Platters; many small Brooks of very good Water; *Guinea* Wheat, Cassado, Pines and Plantains; all things we there Plant, do grow exceedingly, so well as Tobacco; the Corn, Pease, and Beans, cut but away the Stalk, young sprigs will grow, and so bear Fruit for many Years together, without any more Planting; the Isle is overgrown with Wood or great Reeds, those Woods which are soft are exceeding light and full of Pitch, and those that are hard and great, they are as hard to cut as Stone.

{MN} *Fruits and Trees.*

{MN} Mr. *John Powel* came thither the 40th of *August* 1627. with forty five Men, where we stayed three Weeks, and then returning, left behind us about an Hundred People, and his Son *John Powel* for his Deputy, as Governour; but there have been so many Factions amongst them, I cannot from so many variable Relations, give you any certainty for their orderly Government: for all those Plenties, much misery they have endured, in regard of their weakness at their Landing, and long stay without supplies; therefore those that go thither, it were good they carry good Provision with them; but the Isle is most healthful, and all things Planted do increase abundantly; and by this time there is, and now a going, about the number of fifteen or sixteen Hundred People.

{MN} *Their numbers.*

Sir *William Curtine,* and Captain *John Powel,* were the first and chief Adventurers to the Planting this fortunate Isle; which had been oft frequented by Men of War to refresh themselves, and set up their Shallopes; being so far remote from the rest of the Isles, they never were troubled with any of the *Indies.* Harbours they have none, but exceeding good Rodes, which with a small Charge, might be very well Fortified; it doth Ebb and Flow four or five foot, and they cannot perceive that there hath ever been any Hericano in that Isle.

From the Relations of Captain *John White,* and Captain *Wolverstone.*

CHAPTER. XXVII.

The first Plantations of the Isle of Mevis.

{MN-1} BECAUSE I have ranged and lived amongst those Islands, what my Authors cannot tell me, I think it no great error in helping them to tell it my self. In this little Isle of *Mevis,* more than twenty Years ago, I have remained a great time together, to Wood and Water and refresh my Men; it is all Woody, but by the Sea-side Southward, there are Sands like Downs, where a Thousand Men may quarter themselves Conveniently; but in most places the Wood groweth close to the Water side, at a high Water mark, and in some places so thick of a soft spungy Wood like a wild Fig-tree, you cannot get through it, but by making your way with Hatchets, or Fauchions: whether it was the dew of those Trees, or of some others, I am not certain, but many of our Men became so tormented with a burning swelling all over their Bodies, they seemed like scalded Men, and near Mad with Pain; {MN-2} here we found a great Pool wherein bathing themselves they found much ease; and finding it fed with a Pleasant small stream that came out of the Woods, we found the head half a Mile within the Land distilling from many Rocks, by which they were well cured in two or three days. Such factions here we had, as commonly attend such Voyages, that a pair of Gallows were made, but Captain *Smith* for whom they were intended, could not be perswaded to use them; but not any one of the inventors, but their lives by Justice fell into his Power to determine of at his Pleasure, whom with much Mercy he favoured, that most basely and unjustly have betrayed him.

{MN-1} *The Description of the Isle.*

{MN-2} *The Bath.*

{MN} The last Year 1628. Mr. *Littleton* with some others, got a Patent of the Earl of *Carlisle* to Plant the Isle called the *Barbadoes*, thirty Leagues Northward of St. *Christophers;* which by report of their Informers, and Undertakers, for the excellency of the Pleasantness thereof, they called *Dulcina,* but when they came there, they found it such a Barren Rock they left it; altho they were told as much before, they would not believe it, perswading themselves those contradicters would get it for themselves, was thus by their cunning Opinion, the deceivers of themselves; for seeing it lie conveniently for their purpose in a Map, they had not Patience to know the goodness or badness, the inconvenience nor probability of the Quantity nor Quality; which error doth predominate in most of our homebred Adventurers, that will have all things as they conceit and would have it; and the more they are contradicted, the more hot they are; but you may see by many Examples in the general History, how difficult a matter it is, to gather the Truth from amongst so many Foreign and several Relations, except you have exceeding good experience both of the Countries People, and their Conditions; and those ignorant undertakings, have been the greatest hindrance of all those Plantations.

{MN} *A great misfortune.*

{MN} At last because they would be absolute, they came to *Mevis,* a little Isle by St. *Christophers;* where they seated themselves, well furnished with all necessaries, being about the Number of an Hundred, and since increased to an Hundred and fifty Persons, whereof many were old Planters of St. *Christophers;* especially Mr. *Anthony Hinton,* and Mr. *Edward Tompson.* But because all those Isles for the most part are so capable to produce, and in Nature like each other, let this discourse serve for the description of them all. Thus much concerning those Plantations, which now after all this time, loss and charge, should they be abandon'd, suppressed, and dissolved, were most lamentable; and surely seeing they all strive so much about this Tobacco, and that the Fraught thereof, and other charges are so great, and so open to any Enemy by that Commodity they cannot long subsist.

{MN} *Their Numbers.*

And it is a wonder to me to see such Miracles and Mischiefs in Men; how greedily they pursue to dispossess the Planters of the Name of Christ Jesus, yet say they are Christians, when so much of the World is unpossessed; yea, and better Land than they so much strive for, murthering so many Christians, burning and spoiling so many Cities, Villages and Countries, and subverting so many Kingdoms, when so much lieth wait, or only possessed by a few poor Savages, that more serve the Devil for fear, than God for love; whose Ignorance we pretend to reform, but Covetousness, Humours, Ambition, Faction, and Pride hath so many Instruments, we perform very little to any purpose; nor is there either Honour or Profit to be got by any that are so vile, to undertake the subversion, or hinderance of any honest intended Christian Plantation.

{MN} Now to conclude the Travels and Adventures of Captain *Smith;* how first he Planted *Virginia* and was let ashoar with about an Hundred Men in the wild Woods; how he was taken Prisoner by the Savages, by the King of *Pamaunke* tied to a Tree to be shot to death, led up and down their Country to be shewed for a wonder; fatted as he thought, for a Sacrifice for their Idol, before whom they conjured him three days, with strange Dances and

Invocations, then brought him before their Emperor *Powhatan*, that commanded him to be slain; how his Daughter *Pocahontas* saves his life, returned him to *James* Town, relieved him and his famished Company, which was but eight and thirty to possess those large Dominions; how he discovered all the several Nations, upon the Rivers falling into the Bay of *Chisapeacke;* flung near to death with a most Poisoned taile of a Fish called Stingray: how *Powhatan* out of his Country took the Kings of *Pamaunke* and *Paspahegh* Prisoners, forced thirty nine of those Kings to pay him contribution, subjected all the Savages: how *Smith* was blown up with Gun-powder, and returned for *England* to be cured.

{MN} *Certain exploits of Captain* Smith.

Also how he brought our New *England* to the subjection of the Kingdom of Great *Britain;* his fights with the Pirats, left alone amongst a many *French* men of Warr, and his Ship ran from him; his Sea-fights for the *French* against the *Spaniards;* their bad usage of him; how in *France* in a little Boat he escaped them; was adrift all such a stormy Night at Sea by himself, when thirteen *French* Ships were split, or driven on shoar by the Isle of *Ree*, the General and most of his Men drowned, when God, to whom be all Honour and Praise, brought him safe on shoar to all their Admirations that escaped; you may read at large in his General History of *Virginia*, the *Summer Isles*, and *New England.*

CHAPTER. XXVIII.

The bad Life, Qualities and Conditions of Pirates; and how they taught the Turks and Moors to become men of Warr.

AS IN ALL LANDS where there are many People, there are some Thieves, so in all Seas much frequented, there are some Pirates; the most Ancient within the Memory of threescore Years, was one *Callis*, who most refreshed himself upon the Coast of *Wales; Clinton* and *Purser* his Companions, who grew famous till Queen *Elizabeth* of Blessed Memory, hanged them at *Wapping; Flemming* was as expert and as much sought for as they, yet such a Friend to his Country, that discovering the *Spanish Armado*, he voluntarily came to *Plimouth*, yielded himself freely to my Lord Admiral, and gave him notice of the *Spaniards* coming; which good warning came so happily and unexpectedly, that he had his Pardon, and a good Reward; some few Pirates there then remained; notwithstanding it is incredible how many great and rich Prizes the little Barques of the West Country daily brought home, in regard of their small Charge; {MN} for there are so many difficulties in a great Navy, by Wind and Weather, Victual, Sickness, losing and finding one another, they seldom defray half the charge: But for the Grace, State and Defence of the Coast and narrow Seas, a great Navy is most necessary, but not to Attempt any far Voyage, except there be such a Competent flock, they want not wherewith to furnish and supply all things with expedition; but to the purpose.

{MN} *The difficulties of a great Navy.*

{MN} After the death of our most Gracious Queen Elizabeth of Blessed Memory, our Royal King *James*, who from his Infancy had Reigned in Peace with all Nations; had no imployment for those Men of Warr, so that those that were Rich relied with that they had; those that were poor and had nothing but from hand to Mouth, turned Pirates; some, because they became slighted of those for whom they had got much Wealth; some for that they could not get their Due; some that had lived bravely, would not abase themselves to Poverty; some vainly, only to get a name; others for Revenge, Covetousness, or as ill; and as they found themselves more and more oppressed, their Passions increasing with discontent, made them turn Pirates.

{MN} *What occasioneth Pirates.*

{MN} Now because they grew hatefull to all *Christian* Princes, they retired to Barbary, where altho' there be not many good Harbours, but *Tunis, Argier, Sally, Mamora,* and *Tituane,* there are many convenient Rodes, or the open Sea, which is their chief Lordship: For their best Harbours *Massalqueber,* the Towns of *Oran, Mellila, Tangier,* and *Ceuta,* within the Streights, are possessed by the *Spaniards;* without the Streights they have also *Arzella* and *Mazagan; Mamora* they have likewise lately taken, and Fortified. *Ward* a poor *English* Sailer, and *Dansker* a *Dutchman,* made first here their Marts; when the *Moors* knew scarce how to sail a Ship; *Bishop* was Ancient and did little hurt; but *Easton* got so much as made himself a Marquess in *Savoy;* and *Ward* lived like a Bashay in *Barbary;* those were the first that taught the *Moors* to be Men of War. *Gennings, Harris, Tompson,* and divers others were taken in Ireland, a Coast they much frequented, and died at *Wapping. Haws, Bough, Smith, Walsingham, Ellis, Collins, Sawkwel, Wollingstone, Barrow, Wilson, Sayres,* and divers others, all these were Captains amongst the Pirates, whom King *James* Mercifully Pardon'd; and was it not strange, a few of those should command the Seas. Notwithstanding the *Malteses,* the Pope, *Florentines, Genoeses, French, Dutch* and *Engish,* Gallies and Men of War, they Would rob before their Faces, and even at their own Ports, yet seldom more than three, four, five, or six in a Fleet: many times they had very good Ships, and well Man'd, but commonly in such Factions amongst themselves, and so Riotous, Quarrellous, Treacherous, Blasphemous and Villainous, it is more than a wonder they could so long continue, to do so much Mischief; and all they got, they basely consumed it amongst *Jews, Turks, Moors,* and Whores.

{MN} *Their chief Rendezvous.*

The best was, they would seldom go to Sea, so long as they could possibly live on shoar, being compiled of *English, French, Dutch* and *Moors,* (but very few *Spaniards* or *Italians*) commonly running one from another, till they became so disjointed, disordered, debauched, and miserable, {MN} that the *Turks* and *Moors* began to command them as Slaves, and force them to instruct them in their best skill, which many an accursed Runnagado, or *Christian* turned *Turk* did, till they have made those Sally-men or *Moors* of *Barbary* so Powerful as they be, to the Terror of all the Streights, and many times they take Purchase in the Main Ocean, yea sometimes in the narrow Seas in *England,* and those are the most cruel Villains in *Turky* or *Barbary;* whose Natives are very Noble, and of good Natures, in comparison of them.

{MN} *Renegados.*

{MN} To conclude, The Misery of a Pirate, (altho' many are sufficient Seamen as any) yet in regard of his superfluity, you shall find it such, that any wise Man would rather live amongst wild Beasts, than them; therefore let all unadvised Persons take heed they entertain that quality; and I could how wish Merchants, Gentlemen, and all Setters forth of Ships, not to be sparing of a Competent Pay, nor true Payment; for neither Soldiers nor Seamen can live without Means, but necessity will force them to steal; and when they are once entered into that Trade, they are hardly reclaimed. Those Titles of Seamen and Soldiers, have been most worthily honoured and esteemed, but now regarded for the most part, but as the scum of the World; regain therefore your wonted Reputations and endeavour rather to Adventure to those fair Plantations of our English Nation; which however in the beginning were scorned contemned, yet now you see how many Rich and Gallant People come from thence, who went thither as Poor as any Soldier or Sailer, and gets more in one Year, than you by Piracy in seven. I intreat you therefore to consider how many Thousands yearly go thither; also how many Ships and Sailers are imployed to Transport them, and what Custom they Yearly pay to our most Royal King Charles, whole Prosperity and his Kingdom's good, I humbly beseech the Immortal God to preserve and increase.

{MN} *Advertisements for Wild heads.*

FINIS.

Milton Keynes UK
Ingram Content Group UK Ltd.
UKHW031200241024
450188UK00004B/349